UP FROM DOWN

How to Recover from Life-Changing Adverse Events

ERIC PFEIFFER, M.D.

BALBOA.
PRESS

A DIVISION OF HAY HOUSE

Balboa Press books may be ordered through booksellers or by contacting:

Balboa Press
A Division of Hay House
1663 Liberty Drive
Bloomington, IN 47403
www.balboapress.com
1 (877) 407-4847

Because of the dynamic nature of the Internet, any web addresses or links contained in this book may have changed since publication and may no longer be valid. The views expressed in this work are solely those of the author and do not necessarily reflect the views of the publisher, and the publisher hereby disclaims any responsibility for them.

The author of this book does not dispense medical advice or prescribe the use of any technique as a form of treatment for physical, emotional, or medical problems without the advice of a physician, either directly or indirectly. The intent of the author is only to offer information of a general nature to help you in your quest for emotional and spiritual well-being. In the event you use any of the information in this book for yourself, which is your constitutional right, the author and the publisher assume no responsibility for your actions.

This book is a work of non-fiction. Unless otherwise noted, the author and the publisher make no explicit guarantees as to the accuracy of the information contained in this book and in some cases, names of people and places have been altered to protect their privacy.

Any people depicted in stock imagery provided by Getty Images are models, and such images are being used for illustrative purposes only.
Certain stock imagery © Getty Images.

Print information available on the last page.

ISBN: 978-1-9822-1730-3 (sc)
ISBN: 978-1-9822-1729-7 (hc)
ISBN: 978-1-9822-1728-0 (e)

Library of Congress Control Number: 2018914378

Balboa Press rev. date: 12/06/2018

DEDICATION

This book is dedicated
to my wife, Natasha,
and to my three sons:
Eric, Michael, and Mark.
They have been the sunshine and the inspiration of my life.

CONTENTS

FOREWORD

Doctor Eric Pfeiffer is a man of wisdom who can guide you through the difficulties of change. He knows the ropes, so to speak, and will be the light in the lighthouse of transition to bring you into safe harbor. He himself has known the challenge of illness: during his time of authoring this very book he was faced with cancer treatment. He had to create a plan for success to get through the processes and moments of exhaustion and suffering. He is a champion to me and I trust his time-proven steps and ability to show you the truth that life is an adventure and there is more to you than you know. You are stronger than you think.

Every challenge comes with a gift. Read his book and allow it to grow you into a stronger you and into a greater fullness of life. When life feels overwhelming and you want to give up -- stop and ponder his words. Dr. Pfeiffer will show you how to tap into resilience and find the next step into a fulfilling life. I'd trust this man with my life and I encourage you to allow his knowledge to change you and transform you in your dark hours.

Rainbow Abegg, Professional Life Coach, author, motivational speaker and thriver in the difficulties of life.

INTRODUCTION

Bad Things Happen to Good People, and Everybody Else

No matter how old you are, but especially by your later years, you will experience losses and traumas. You may lose a loved one, experience severe illness, go through a divorce, lose a job, lose financial resources, or lose your home from a fire or hurricane. These events can indeed be life-changing. If you have experienced one or more of them, you may have felt devastated, severely depressed, or unable to function. You may have found it difficult to enjoy life, or to contribute to your family or your community for long periods of time. But it doesn't have to be that way. You can embark on a course of recovery that will help you regain your equilibrium and your momentum. You may even get to "better than before" if you apply the right strategies.

How This Book Will be Helpful to You

This book is designed to help you in two ways: One, is to offer general guidance on what to do in order to cope with any trauma, crisis, or loss: Two, is to offer specific strategies for dealing with the particular adverse event happening to you. These recommendations can apply to you, the reader, or they can help you to assist someone near and dear to you to as they weather their adversity.

The book discusses many different kinds of events, not all of which will happen to you or your loved ones. However these happenings are instructive on how to rebound from any knockdown. Examples of these will be given throughout the book.

How I Came to Focus on the Recovery Process

My most significant experience leading to focusing on the recovery process has been observing hundreds, no, thousands, of caregivers of Alzheimer's patients going through years of caregiving, only to arrive at the end of their caregiver period exhausted, depleted, drained, and barely able to function. I learned that to embark on an active recovery period was an absolute necessity for there to be "life after caregiving."

Similarly, I learned that other life-changing events such as loss of a loved one, loss of a job, loss of finances, and many more life-changing events, left people reeling, directionless, stunned, and impaired in many ways. I contend that a similar recovery process is equally beneficial in those situations. Of course each traumatic event has its own specific consequences and effects. Hence specific techniques geared to these events need to be applied to achieve full recovery.

For whom is this Book Written?

Up from Down is written for you, the reader, who may have experienced one or more of these devastating events, or who has seen someone close to you experience one or more of these calamities. It is also written for the person likely to experience one or more adverse events in the future and who wants to be better prepared. It is written for those who are still struggling with the effects or after-effects of a life-changing event and don't know where to turn for help. *Up from Down* is intended to make a difference in how you cope with life-changing circumstances. It does not offer a passive form of help but one that puts YOU in charge of all the directing and the redirecting that needs to be done. It asks a lot of you, and in turn promises to give back a lot to you. So that is the deal. Are you in? I hope so. You will not regret it. In fact, if things go the best way possible you will come out of the present or a future life-changing event far stronger, wiser, more confident, more creative than ever before. At the least you will limit the negative effects of anything that has come or will come your way. That is my promise to you.

Why this Book had to be Written

Up from Down had to be written to help people get unstuck from the impact of traumas and adverse events. In my 50 years as a physician I have seen people make both successful and unsuccessful adaptations to losses and traumatic events. I am here to share with you some of the successful techniques I have observed and learned, so you the reader need not experience feelings of being overwhelmed, with possible depression, social isolation, and inability to function.

It may be of interest that just as I was beginning to write this book, I was personally hit by one of the most life-changing events: The diagnosis of cancer! I will make reference to my experience with this event at several points throughout the book, as well as devoting a whole chapter to my experience with cancer and cancer treatment.

About the Stories in this Book

Throughout *Up from Down* I will share with you a number of stories to illustrate the possible types of events and the types of recovery strategies that have proven useful. These stories are inspired by the experiences of real people. However, to protect their privacy, their names, plus other identifying information items, have been changed so us not to reveal the identity of the actual individuals involved.

On some topics more than one illustration is included in order to showcase different responses to similar events. In others, no illustrations are presented. In still others, only an illustration is presented, without additional narrative content. The reason for this variability is that individuals are unique and life is irregular; it is not predictable. I hope you will find in these stories someone or more than one person that you can relate to.

How to Read this Book

Up from Down is an inspirational How-to, Self-help, book to help people recover from the depth of despair after being hit by losses and traumas. It can help to get to "good as before" or sometimes, "even better."

When you read *Up from Down*, I hope you will feel free to mark it up with highlight or under-linings when something hits home. This will solidify the information in your mind. For this reason, I hope you will get your own copy of the book, although feel free to recommend it to your local library so more people can benefit from its content.

While you may find that only some topics in this book are of interest to you, I do recommend that you read the entire book, paying special attention to those events affecting you directly. That way you will have resources at the ready when a friend, a loved one, or you yourself confront a situation similar to one addressed herein.

I recommend that you keep this book around for years to come. A second or even a third reading will be more illuminating than your first read, and new events may have happened in the interval, events you never thought would happen to you.

CHAPTER 1

OVERVIEW

In this Chapter I will describe what lies ahead for you, the reader. I plan to show you how to accomplish full recovery, without floundering and without having to go through all the possible useless trials and errors. *Up from Down* is further based on the idea that in order to succeed you must address not just some but all major aspects of your life. So, quite a tall order! The book will teach you how to rebound from life-changing adverse events. However, to do so you need to take some very specific actions.

In Chapter 2 we are going to discuss the absolutely essential steps you must take to achieve full recovery. These steps will give you a systematic plan that you can enact even during the most adverse events. With this essential recovery process in place, you can then *commit* to making recovery your number 1 priority and minimize the aftershocks of residual damage.

In Chapter 3 we are going to discuss a series of general steps which are supportive of recovery. These include maintaining good physical health, good mental health, fitness, and good nutrition. They also include remaining socially connected, allowing your-self pleasurable activities, listening to music, and avoiding negative input—for example, turning off CNN and Fox News. They also include the possibility of taking an afternoon nap, gardening or in some other way reconnecting with nature, developing an attitude of gratitude and maintaining a positive outlook on life. In addition it may be useful to plan something to look forward to in the future, journaling about your experience, and staying spiritually connected. The chapter concludes with an encouraging "You can do it!" declaration.

In the next Chapter we begin our discussion about specific adverse events, and how to cope with them. Thus, in Chapter 4 we will discuss a number of losses that are related to income and money: loss of one's job, loss of finances, and loss of one's home through a hurricane, fire, or flood.

In regard to the loss of one's job we will discuss first of all the need not to panic and not to exaggerate the magnitude of the adverse event. Then we can come to consider this disaster as an opportunity for new perspectives and new lifestyles. We then discuss considering a variety of types of replacement jobs. This is followed by a discussion of alternatives to a replacement job, such as running one's own business or entering one of the arts. Herbert's and Paul's stories illustrate a number of significant points in the journey towards replacing a lost job.

In regard to recovery from a financial loss, John's story is illustrative of the opportunities presented after a financial loss that can help to rebuild financial security.

In regard to the loss of one's home through a hurricane, Mel and Lisa's story illustrate both the impact of such a loss as well as how to recover from it.

In Chapter 5 we discuss recovery from some physical ailments. These include recovery from a stroke, recovery from a heart attack, and recovery from loss of hearing and from loss of vision.

Recovery from a stroke requires rapid medical attention after the stroke, followed by vigorous physical, occupational, or speech therapy, depending on the disability caused by the stroke. The story of Tom is illustrative of a relatively good though not perfect outcome.

Hearing loss is common as people grow older. Appropriate hearing aids can provide substantial improvement of hearing capacity. In some cases even cochlear implants are needed to restore hearing. If hearing cannot be restored the learning of sign language is appropriate.

Loss of vision can be caused by a number or factors: diabetes, cataracts, and nerve damage. Again, appropriate eye glasses, cataract surgery, and excellent control of diabetes is needed. If all of these fail, the person will have to use his remaining senses to make up for the loss of vision.

In Chapter 6 we discuss recovery from mental illnesses. Those discussed include depression, anxiety, alcoholism, schizophrenia and post-traumatic stress disorder.

Depression is probably the most common of mental disorders. It is characterized by sadness, pessimism, loss of interest and sometimes suicidal ideas. It can be treated with psychotherapy alone or with psychotherapy and antidepressant medication. Most depressions respond to active treatment, at least in part if not completely. Anxiety, alcoholism and schizophrenia treatments are also discussed, as are post-traumatic stress disorders or PTSD.

In Chapter 7 we discuss recovery from a cancer diagnosis and from cancer treatment. This is my own personal story. I was diagnosed with cancer of the tongue, with metastasis to two near-by lymph nodes. I was treated with intense radiation therapy and chemotherapy, and became cancer free. However, the treatment left me with a number of problems: Loss of taste, loss of energy, loss of weight, and a low blood count. Gradual recovery from these side effects of treatment is discussed.

In Chapter 8 we discuss recovery from having a loved one diagnosed with Alzheimer's disease. This can have a tremendous impact on a spouse or other family member. Not only will he or she see the one they love gradually deteriorate, but he or she may have to take on the caregiver role. The caregiver role may last anywhere from two to twenty years, depending on the rate of progression of the patient's disease. The story of Harry, who is a model caregiver, illustrates many of the issues involved in having a spouse diagnosed with Alzheimer's disease.

In Chapter 9 we discuss recovery from the death of loved ones. Here we discuss the impact of sudden death of a spouse, the impact of the death of an adult child, death of a spouse by murder, and loss of an unborn child. Numerous stories illustrate the various aspects of these losses and a variety of approaches to dealing with these losses.

In Chapter 10 we discuss recovery from caregiving, specifically recovery from caregiving of an Alzheimer's patient. However, caregivers of family members with other diseases or disabilities are also discussed. It should be noted that seeing the devastation of being a long time caregiver was part of the motivation for writing this book. A number of stories illustrate the many features of the exhausted caregiver.

Now that you have been given an overview of what lies ahead, you are ready to delve into Essential Steps towards Recovery.

CHAPTER 2

ESSENTIAL STEPS TOWARD RECOVERY

In this chapter we are going to discuss actions which an individual can take which are essential in the recovery process regardless of the specific nature of the adverse event, be it trauma, severe stress, loss of a loved one, or some other form of disaster.

The next few paragraphs will describe actions which are vital to an effective recovery. They include a thorough objective assessment of one's situation, advice not to catastrophize one's situation, assessing the limits of the damage that has been done, and then looking for the silver lining in the situation.

Next, it is important to make a **commitment** to undertake the recovery process, and then making it the number one priority in your life. After that there is real value in looking for and joining a support group of people who have had a similar experience to yours.

Begin with an Objective Assessment of your Situation

It is important to start with an objective assessment of your situation. After an adverse event occurs people tend to catastrophize their situation, feeling that all areas of their lives have been negatively affected. But this is in fact not true. Numerous major areas of your life will have remained intact, and may be a great source of gratitude. For instance, the sudden loss of a loved one in general will not affect the status of your health, your wealth, your social connectedness, or any number of other facets of your life. You may not be able to make such an assessment by yourself, but with the help of a trusted friend, a confidant, or even a professional advisor, you may be able to discover that the impact of the adverse event is, in fact, limited to specific areas of your life. You can then target those areas for rebuilding.

Resist the Tendency to Catastrophize

It is important to resist the tendency to exaggerate the impact of the event. Keep in mind that not everything has been destroyed. The impact of the event will not last forever. There may be things you can do to lessen the impact of the event, or, in some instances, to replace a loss which has occurred.

Take note of what has been left Intact by the Event

Also, observe with gratitude all those things that have NOT changed but have remained intact. You may still have your health, or your home, or your family and friends; you may still have your job and your ability to adapt. Be grateful for the strengths, connections, and abilities that you still possess.

Look for the Silver Lining

Even in the most difficult of situations there is often a silver lining, although it may take time and effort to see it. It may consist of no longer having to provide care, needing only one car in the family, opportunity to resume activities suspended by the preceding events, or something that only you can discover. But by all means, search for it!

Throughout this book evidence of such silver linings will be presented. Sometimes they will be highlighted by a section called "What is the possible silver lining?" in this situation. At other times they will just be presented within the text of that topic.

Remember, it is Difficult to be Objective

It is difficult to be objective when you have just been traumatized. Therefore I recommend that you get some help with this from a trusted person such as a close friend, a confidante, or a professional counsellor. Or you might get together with people who have been through a similar experience recently, i.e. by joining a support group: it will immediately make it clear that you are not alone. And you will quickly be enveloped by the warmth of your fellow group members.

Your Next Step is to commit to Undertaking a Recovery Process

You will need to make a real commitment to engage in a recovery process from the adverse event, and then implement the plan for recovery. Without that commitment you will not be able to right yourself, and your life will continue in substantial misery. But with it you can reach full recovery, and if you are lucky, you can achieve greater things than you ever have before.

Make Recovery Your Number One Priority

You should certainly make recovery a priority in your life. No, actually you should make it your number one priority. It is that important.

Without a systematic plan for recovery from a major adverse event the outcome is likely to be more detrimental than need be. Without such a commitment the premise that you can actually benefit from such an event will also go unfulfilled. There is no doubt that an intentional recovery process will minimize any residual damage.

Find and Join a Support Group, if Available

As I mentioned earlier, one of the most useful things you can and do is to find and join a support group for people who have undergone experiences similar to yours. You will see that your situation is not unique, but that it is not your fault. In addition you will learn from others going through the recovery process how to deal with specific situations or circumstances. You will also enlarge your social circle in this way, and at times you will also contribute useful information to someone else, some new insights to whatever loss the person has experienced.

I became convinced of the enormous value of support groups as they related to caregiving in Alzheimer's disease. But the benefits can be equally great for support groups related to other events: stroke: loss of child; loss of a limb, or loss of a job. Support groups are not general; they are always focused on individuals with a common event or calamity In short, there is no such thing as a "support group for recovery." But do find the support group for people dealing with the same or similar problem you are facing. If none exists, you could always start one, and invite other people to join you in this endeavor. It has to be specific. It has to be led by someone who is deeply knowledgeable about the topic, either by a professional in that field (e.g.: physician, psychologist, nurse, or social worker) or a lay person who is thoroughly steeped in the subject matter, or better yet, by both a professional and a lay leader. We will return to the issue of support groups in a number of the specific topics on adverse events below.

CHAPTER 3

GENERAL STEPS SUPPORTIVE OF RECOVERY

In this chapter we are going to discuss activities which are generally supportive of the recovery process. They are also basic to living a successful life in general, regardless of adverse events and traumas. Give them a try!

Attaining and/or Maintaining Good Health

Good health is necessary for anything you want or need to do. What is needed to maintain good health? First, you must have a competent and accessible primary care physician who will serve as the organizer for all your healthcare needs. He or she will provide your general healthcare needs, order basic lab work, obtain required x-rays and provide needed immunizations. He or she will be the first to see you when a new health care problem or a new diagnosis pops up. You must choose someone who is convinced that any new health problem requires full evaluation and treatment aimed at alleviating the problem altogether (such as an infection) or to minimize the functional impairment caused by the disease (such as with diabetes, heart failure or hearing loss). To be consistent with our theme of recovery, it also requires the completion of a full course of rehabilitation following a stroke, hip fracture, or other injury.

Attaining and Maintaining Good Mental Health

A huge amount has been written about this topic. For our purposes, however, only a few major points need to be made. In many ways, all of the techniques described in this section contribute to mental health (i.e. physical health, fitness, a positive attitude, an attitude of gratitude). However I want to add the need for psychological or psychiatric intervention if specific mental health symptoms occur. Your life-changing events may trigger depression, anxiety, panic, or even psychotic states which require prompt and effective psychological and/or pharmacological treatment beyond that provided by your primary care doctor.

Becoming or Staying Socially Connected

Becoming or remaining socially connected is also needed for complete recovery. Your connections may include family members, friends, church or other social group memberships, activity groups (such as walking together for fitness: more on that shortly) or other interest groups such as book clubs, choirs, bridge, volunteer activities etc.

Maintaining Fitness and Good Nutrition

In order to fully recover from major life-changing events one must be or become fit and well-nourished. This means you must implement some kind of fitness program that you regularly pursue, such as walking, dancing, gym exercises, yoga or tai-chi. This will give you the energy to do all the other activities needed in your pursuit of recovery. Similarly, good nutrition will be the other element for assuring a good energy level throughout the day. This may mean following a Mediterranean diet, a paleo-diet, a low carbohydrate diet or, at its simplest level, "No sugar, and no wheat." This will accomplish not being or becoming overweight. Obesity is not consistent with either successful aging or full recovery.

Allowing Yourself to Experience Pleasurable Activities

Many people dealing with grief feel that it is wrong to seek or to have fun. *Au contraire!* Participating in pleasurable activities or seeking out pleasurable activities is just the ticket to a faster recovery. A trip to the beach, a dinner out with friends, an occasional show, or a spontaneous cocktail party is just what I would prescribe. On a grander scale, and if money is no object, consider a brief visit to San Francisco or New York City, or a cruise in the Caribbean or the Mediterranean. You will find that any one of these can have enormous restorative value.

Turn up the Music

Your choice of music (classical, rock and roll, country music, popular, music, opera, or whatever your choice) can bring peaceful distraction from dealing with whatever problem has happened. It can be mere background activity to whatever you are doing, such as housework or writing. Or it can be an activity on its own. One can listen to music over dinner, or outdoors, or while taking a walk. Music can calm your soul, leaving your worries in the background or forgotten altogether.

Turn off CNN, FOX News and Other Loud Voices

For a period of time, turn off the TV, especially the evening news which tends to be filled with disturbing reports and images. Since there is little you can do about these events, not hearing about them for a while will do you no harm. Also local news tends to be filled with sensational stories, especially reports of local murders, regardless of where you are in the United States. Listening to the news will not improve your state of mind or your readiness to cope with your own circumstances. So turn off the local news as well. I am not suggesting you cancel your subscription to television, but reserve it for specifically selected programs.

Take a Brief Afternoon Nap

I recommend a brief (30 to 45 minute) nap each afternoon when you may be at the low point of your energy. It will not distract from your ability to sleep at night, and you will awake refreshed and full of energy. You can easily do this at home. Trying to do it at work would require agreement from your supervisor that this is a good idea, and a place to rest other than at your office desk. In your office, too, you will return to your tasks with new vigor and enthusiasm, and your productivity will be renewed.

Reconnect with Nature

The curative and creative nature of nature can do wonders for a grieving person. You can take a walk in the park, enjoy an afternoon by the seashore, or watch a sunrise or a sunset over the water somewhere in your neighborhood. It can elevate your mood and allow new and creative ideas to flow.

An Attitude of Gratitude

In the midst of misery over what has just gone wrong, cultivate an attitude of gratitude for all the good things that are still in your life. Usually, the adverse event has affected only a small fraction of your life, while many other areas remain intact. It is useful to dwell on these, one at a time, to gain a perspective on how much good still remains in your life. Your health may still be good; your intelligence will remain intact; your ability to cope will be proven over and over again, even though you may doubt this for a while. Just having a comfortable home may be a great comfort to you. You need to express special gratitude for supportive family and friends. Access to nature remains available. Consider keeping a gratitude journal where you record newly discovered areas of your life for which you are grateful. It can make it easier for you to cope with adverse events.

Maintaining a Positive Attitude

Along with gratitude, strive for a generally positive attitude during your recovery journey. It will make every task you face that much easier, and you will accomplish more. You may want to do this by using positive affirmation statements, speaking with friends or family members who are supportive, listening to music or engaging in physical activities such as walking, or dancing, or calisthenics. Do avoid people with negative attitudes if at all possible. Whatever you do to elevate your mood will help you to be successful. This will include celebrating the occurrence of small accomplishments alone or, better yet, in the company of others.

Positively Look Forward to Something in Your Future

It is vitally important that you have something positive to look forward to in your future. It might be a visit with your children, a trip to Cape Cod, a theater weekend in New York City, or whatever might turn your fancy. Visualize it in detail. Put it on your calendar; get tickets for it right now, even though it may be several months from now. Get brochures of the area you are planning on visiting or get the theater schedule; anything to make it more real, more visual in your mind. Allow yourself to feel ahead of time what a curtain call, or a swim in the ocean, or the taste of a rum drink, might be like. Make it come to life, whenever you need a lift from your depression or grief or disappointment, and you will feel better. Experience the joy of the future event right now! Picture it! Hear it! Taste it!

Stay Spiritually Connected

Your spiritual connection can provide a consistent and powerful resource and substantial boost and solace. You may participate in formal religious activities, or in such other practices as mindfulness, meditation, yoga, or just deep breathing. Connecting with one's inner self through any of these activities will encourage attitudes of peace, joy, and love.

Gardening

If you have any plot of land, be it a back yard, a front yard, a community garden, or even a kitchen window sill or balcony, you can give gardening a chance. Seeing a plant growing and flowering is a wonderful experience. In addition, plants can attract butterflies and butterflies can attract birds. You could put a bird bath or a bird feeder in the middle of your plantings for your entertainment. In addition, gardening can provide a certain amount of exercise for you which you will hardly notice. You owe it to yourself.

Journaling about Your Experience

Many people going through adverse circumstances have found that journaling about the experience is beneficial in quite a number of ways: It helps to clarify what you are going through. It provides you with perspective over time. It invites reflection like nothing else. It is an outlet for your emotions. It is comforting to entrust one's thoughts to "Dear Diary."

You Can Do It!

Above all else, please understand that you must and can do it! Let this be my pep talk to you. You must approach recovery from any life-changing event with vigor and with the absolute conviction that you can adjust to whatever has happened. Look, you have done so up till now. This is just a little harder, requiring a little more creativity, a little more endurance, a little more blood, sweat and tears. You will be well rewarded.

Your Unique Road to Recovery

While I have described a lengthy series of efforts which can help you in the recovery process, you may have discovered one or more activities that have been equally helpful that uniquely suit your character, personality, or situation. I would like to invite you to share any such additional approaches with me at epfeiffe@health.usf.edu.

And now you are ready for reading about the first of the adverse events discussed in this book.

CHAPTER 4

RECOVERY FROM THE LOSS OF A JOB, FINANCIAL LOSS, OR LOSS OF ONE'S HOME

In this chapter we are going to discuss a number of adverse events that are related to money and finances. The first of these relates to the loss of one's job.

Recovery from Loss of One's Job

During the financial crisis of 2008 a large number of individuals lost their jobs unexpectedly. These job losses were not based on poor performance or malfeasance but were necessitated by cutting back expenditures from part of an organization in order to allow the rest of the organization to survive. To say that most of these individuals were not prepared for such an event would be an understatement. It included laborers, blue collar workers, professionals, and executives. It would be difficult to say which group of workers were the most devastated by the event: they all had their props knocked out from under them. Several case illustrations will show the range and scope of reactions to the unexpected loss of a job.

Apart from the general instructions previously discussed in Chapters 2 and 3, there are some specific bits of advice that apply in this situation:

Don't panic; don't exaggerate

It is easy to say, "Don't panic; don't exaggerate," but it is much more difficult to do so. Realistically, only a single, if major, area of one's life has been affected. However it may feel like all of one's life has come to an end. Some people may have stored up an emergency fund for just such a situation. Others have only a month's worth of pay in the bank, and a few bills in their wallet. It will be best to make a sober and objective assessment of what the change in job status means, and then begin to formulate a plan for either finding another job or else finding another source of income, such as opening one's own business, or becoming a consultant in your area of expertise.

Assess the situation

This may best be done with another trusted person, a colleague, a confidant, a similarly unemployed person, or even a professional counselor. It is important to assess what remains intact.

We can assume that your skill set remains intact. Unless the loss of job was a firing for cause, your reputation would seem to stay intact. Less certain is your self-esteem which may be at least somewhat bruised. Your social and professional network should probably still be somewhat intact, if diminished.

Disaster as Opportunity

You need to assess whether you simply want to replace the previous job, or whether you want to take this as an opportunity to explore any number of new aspects. This could involve an entirely new area geographically or occupationally. Thus, you may wish to consider one or more of the following:

- Consider similar jobs
- Consider related but differing jobs
- Consider entirely different jobs
- Consider starting your own business
- Consider running an internet-based business
- Consider retiring early if enough financial resources or reserves are available

Thus, while losing your job definitely qualifies as an adverse event, it can also constitute the silver lining, namely the chance to explore other opportunities and to pursue unfulfilled dreams about how to conduct one's life. So it will be important not to simply reach for a quick solution but to take some time to possibly consider and pursue other life directions. Here are a few suggestions:

Consider Similar Jobs

A first and logical approach to finding a new job is to consider similar jobs to the one just lost: the expertise is there; you know the field; you probably still have sufficient contacts who might be aware of available positions with other firms or organizations; and using these connections to introduce yourself to the possible new organization rather than doing this through cold calling.

Consider Related but Different Jobs

You might also take this occasion to consider a somewhat different line of work. Let us say you were let go from a job in wine merchandising: consider merchandising in electronics instead. Or, if you were let go from a job at a bank, you might seek a job in real estate.

Consider Entirely Different Jobs

Or, you might consider an entirely different line of employment: for instance, going into sales, running for public office, or entering the religious ministry, to show just how far-flung such exploration can go. You, I am sure, you can think of many more logical or even more uncommon possibilities.

Consider Running Your Own Business

So much for considering other jobs. This might be the occasion to no longer work for someone else but to go into business for yourself. You could use your work skills to become a consultant, or to start a niche business of some kind, or to simply learn an entirely new set of skills and going into business with that. Here you should be led by your dreams, your passion or your early ambitions which were set aside as you took a relatively standard job.

Consider Running an Internet-Based Business

Over the last several years a whole new area for income generation has opened up: the world-wide web. You could consider starting an internet business, using your professional skills from your previous job. Or you could use newly acquired skills, such as public speaking on the topic of your expertise or your passion, advertised on the internet. Other possibilities on the internet are giving live seminars, individual and group consultations, blogging, selling informational products you have created, such as books, and many more possibilities. It might be worth your while looking into this arena.

Give One of the Arts a Shot

You may have heard of Grandma Moses who began a successful painting career late in life. You can try painting or sculpture. You can start to write novels, or how-to-books, or decide just to devote yourself to writing poetry (but be warned that poetry doesn't pay). Again, rely on your dreams and what you had always hoped to be able to do.

Get SBA Loans to Start Your Business

Even the government wants to help you. The Small Business Administration offers loans for start-up costs for new businesses.

You May Need Professional Help with Emotional Problems

It is not unusual for individuals who suddenly lose their job to develop emotional problems. If so, you may need to get professional psychological help for emotional problems, such as depression, anxiety or panic disorders. Or you may wish to look for and join a support group for people who have lost their jobs. There you can learn what others are doing to find new employment, and can certainly benefit from the camaraderie of others in the same boat.

How long does it take to find a new job or other income-producing activity?

Best case scenario, you have enough in emergency resources to not have to hurry the decision about new employment. That way you can take up to six months or worst case, even a year to find alternative sources of income.

Networking

By far the best way of finding re-employment is through networking: staying in touch with professional colleagues, attending meetings, staying in touch by e-mail or telephone, or even by snail mail.

Finally, just a reminder that unemployment insurance is available for someone with involuntary loss of job.

Unemployment insurance can provide for the necessities of life, although generally at a much lower level than your previous compensation.

That is not to say that any of this will come easy. It will certainly be a challenge. But it can represent an amazing opportunity for personal growth.

Herbert's Story:

Herbert was an executive in a real estate firm, and as a result of the recession of 2008 his firm suffered considerable loss of business and had to cut back the number of executives it employed. Herbert was "let go," not because of any deficiency in his work but because the total number of both agents and executives had to be reduced.

Herbert was blind-sided as well as devastated by the event. He wondered what he could have done to avoid his firing, but couldn't come up with anything. And while he did not have sufficient emergency funds to support him during this period, fortunately his wife had a well-paying job and could help to sustain the family for a considerable time. In fact, his wife who had similar connections in the real estate field was able to make a number of contacts for him, one of which resulted in reemployment in a similar executive position to the one from which he had been let go. Thus his period of discomfort was relatively brief for him, and Herbert was able to restart not only his earning but also his charitable activities in the community.

Paul's Story:

    Paul was the Chief Financial Officer of a successful restaurant chain. Its success attracted the attention of a much larger restaurant chain which, after doing is due diligence on Paul's company, purchased Paul's company outright and integrated it into the overall management structure of the larger company. A separate CFO was no longer needed, and Paul was out of a job. He had done nothing wrong; he had not failed in any way other than not seeing this event coming. He had a good reputation, and with the proceeds from the sale of the small portion of stock in the original company to carry him for a few months, he could take time to consider whether he wanted to continue in the same occupation or re-examine his options. He decided to do the latter.

    There were a lot of things to consider: What did his wife think of the idea of his changing jobs altogether, and how would it affect her? Did he want to stay in the same town that he lived in now or relocate to a more favorable climate? He decided he wanted to try to harvest a lesson from the event to share with others. He decided to write a book on the vicissitudes of financial planning in an era of mergers and acquisitions which he did over the next 6 months. He then published his book on Amazon. com, under the title "What Every CFO Ought to Know." The book was a huge success. He was invited to consult with major corporations involved in the merger and acquisitions field. He was invited to speak at several national organizations. He travelled extensively, always offering to take his wife with him to places she too might want to go, sometimes adding two or three days of personal time if the location was something like New Orleans, Southern California, or Miami. Who could complain about that? He invested his considerable income from his new activities with a trusted and proven financial advisor, and made almost as much money in the stock market as from his new business activities. Occasionally he and his wife had dinner at a restaurant of the larger chain that had bought his original company, but with mixed feelings. This is an example of where an adverse circumstance was converted into something better than was before.

Recovery from a Financial Loss

During the recession of 2008 many people lost large amounts of money, anywhere from a few thousand dollars to millions of dollars. As with any loss, the key ingredient in seeking recovery is replacement. This may take considerable amounts of time.

One of the benefits of our tax system is that it allows for carry-over losses from one year to the next. This is where you will probably have the best opportunity to regain capital: Cautiously invest for capital gains, and then offset them against carry-forward losses. No tax, no pain.

John's Story:

John Granger, a successful dentist, had been "playing the market" quite successfully since his college days, based *on the principle of spending less money than he earned, and investing the rest. For many years the market was favorable for his investments and he accumulated a handsome holding amounting to several million dollars. Then came 2008 and the Great Recession, and "poor" John didn't see it coming. He was busy with his practice and didn't have either the time or the knowledge of how to deal with such an event. Along with millions of other individuals he lost about half of his holdings. Beginning in 2009 the market gradually improved, and some of his losses were made right but he nevertheless was a long way from recovering what he had lost. Over several years after 2008 he continued to experience small additional losses until he learned how to be more cautious and build safety features into his investments. He then began to make capital gains from his investments and discovered that capital gains could be off-set against capital losses incurred in 2008 and in subsequent years. And the capital gains were in fact tax free! He found that he had quite a large amount in carry-forward losses from 2008 which allowed him to take these profits free of taxes. This made him eager to try to recover more of his lost fortune, and in 2016 he accrued a $55,000 capital gain, all of which was tax-free. Then in 2017 he became even more aggressive while at the same time being more safety oriented, and he accrued a $250,000.00 capital gain. He is planning to keep doing this until he regains his former fortune.*

Loss of a Home from a Hurricane, a Tornado, Fire, or a Flood

One type of loss more likely to occur in Florida, the Southeast Coast, or the West coast, is a loss of a home from a major hurricane. Loss of a home from a tornado in any part of the country can be similarly devastating. Loss of a home from a fire can of course occur anywhere. And losses from a flood tend to be associated with other weather disasters. The loss of one's home can be monumental because it attacks nearly all aspects of one's life: housing, finances, documents, personal treasures, and a style of life. It is hard to know where to begin in initiating the recovery process.

First one must find temporary housing, assuming one's former home is uninhabitable. Next, one must wait for FEMA to visit the area in order to make a decision as to whether the event qualifies as a national disaster to make additional Federal help available to those affected. Next you will need to deal with the applicable flood insurance program, assuming you have one. Obviously it is even worse if there is no such coverage. Can the home be restored at all or is it a total loss? Next, what all has been lost in the disaster? Clothing, financial records, photographs, personal treasures and mementoes, tools, work gear etc.? Inventorying all that is lost is probably a next important step. Those living in coastal areas now find out why there is a mandatory flood insurance program in place.

One can expect that it will take months or even years to fully recover a habitable home. The psychological reaction to this kind of a loss can be even more extensive. Relocations, recalculations, revisions of one's goals and life style may all be involved. Severe psychological reactions such as depression and post-traumatic stress disorders may occur, especially if the person witnessed the destruction of his or her home.

Mel and Lisa's Story:

Lisa and Mel lived in a comfortable home two blocks off the beach just south of Miami. Hurricane Andrew completely destroyed their home, along with many others in the same area, and the area was declared a national disaster area by FEMA.

Their home was judged to be a total loss and could not be repaired. They decided to move inland and went to Virginia. There they both made and found new friends, new jobs, and a new outlook on life. They spent more time together in their new lovely home, paid for with the proceeds from the Hurricane Insurance. They still visited occasionally with their friends in the Miami area, but their future was clearly going to be in Virginia. However the trauma of the devastation of their home continued to haunt them in nightmares and in daytime flash-backs.

As their children went away to college they were thrown much more together and a number of conflicts blossomed, leading ultimately to a divorce. Lisa remarried happily in Virginia. Mel did not and moved back to Florida where he could practice his passion for boating more easily than he could in inland Virginia. They each remained friends with many of the friends they had when they had been married. They also shared a common interest in their children. Nevertheless the loss of their home from a hurricane had left lasting scars on their lives, their finances, and their children.

. . . .

There you have it: Three examples of how to recover from various financial losses. The lesson from each of these is: **there is a way back.** Active steps are required to accomplish this, but it is possible.

Now on to our next topic: Recovery from some physical ailments.

CHAPTER 5

RECOVERY FROM SOME PHYSICAL AILMENTS

Recovery from a Stroke

Before going on to discuss recovery from a stroke, a great deal can be said about how to prevent a stroke. A stroke is the result of one or more areas of the blood supply to the brain being disrupted, resulting in death of brain tissue and consequent loss of function. These can include paralysis of the limbs on one side or another of the body, slurring or inability to speak, loss of ability to use skilled hand movements, loss of balance and instability. The most important thing in stroke prevention is to assure a healthy cardiovascular status, including normal blood pressure and heart rhythm, normal blood coagulation status and normal heart function. When the cardiovascular status is in healthy condition a stroke is unlikely to occur.

Once a stroke has occurred, the most important advice is to *seek immediate medical attention* at an emergency room so that anticoagulation or surgery can be initiated. Time is of the essence in this regard. Here *minutes count!*

Within a few days it will become clear what function has been affected or lost. It is then time to begin a systematic program of rehabilitation, addressing the specific area of neurological deficit. *Physical therapy* is most useful when weakness or paralysis of one or more of the limbs has occurred. With vigorous therapy other parts of the brain can be taught to take over the function of the lost area, in many cases leading to full or near complete return of function. In a similar way, vigorous and extensive *speech therapy* can lead to relearning of normal speech and speech patterns, so that the person can communicate properly. *Occupational therapy* is the approach to teaching fine muscle movements such as used in cooking or writing, or other complex movement of the hands. One cannot expect things to return to normal just from the passage of time. Vigorous training of alternative brain cell groups is needed to recover full function. And nothing short of full recovery of function should be accepted as the goal of rehabilitation.

In addition, once rehabilitation is under way, it is critical that all the cardiovascular risk factors be addressed and corrected so that another stroke does not occur. This obviously requires the coordination and collaboration of multiple health professionals, supervised by a knowledgeable primary care physician acting as quarterback of the entire proceedings. It also requires the active and diligent participation of the affected patient.

When recovering from a stroke it may also be especially helpful to find and join a stroke recovery support group. The camaraderie of the members, the mutual encouragement, the sharing of small and large victories in recovering functions, can be very encouraging.

Of course not all patients suffering a stroke can expect to restore completely normal functioning. There may be some residual weaknesses that might require the use of a cane, or relearning lost skills with the other hand, for example.

Tom's story:

Tom was a 65 year old construction supervisor who appeared to be in good health. However one day while on the job he suddenly fell over and went into convulsions. Someone called 911 and an ambulance arrived quickly and took him to the nearest hospital. On neurological examination he was shown to have weakness on his right side, with severe weakness of his right leg and lesser weakness of his right arm. Tom was right-handed so that mattered even more. A CAT scan showed blockage of a left vertebral artery. He was started on anticoagulant treatment to prevent further artery clogging. After three more days in the hospital it became clear that his right-sided weakness continued, and he was transferred to a rehabilitation facility for physical therapy. His speech was intact.

He engaged in vigorous physical therapy for about four weeks, and was then discharged to continue exercises for his right arm and leg at home. Tom was eager to recover enough function to be able to drive again. After another month of exercises at home he accomplished this goal and was declared safe to drive by his doctor, to his great relief and that of his wife. He did not return to work, however, and took retirement as he was of the right age to be able to do so.

It turned out that he had had moderately elevated blood pressure before his stroke, and this was treated by his doctor to prevent any recurrence. He also was placed on a daily baby aspirin to keep his blood flowing properly. He had to learn to do some small hand movements with his left hand, which he was able to do, as his right hand had not returned to full strength and agility.

What is the silver lining here?

Tom received quick and early treatment for his stroke. He received appropriate physical therapy for his disability. Tom participated vigorously in his own treatment, and was able to return to near-normal functioning. Incidentally this led to his retirement, and he began to make plans on what to do in his retirement years. His mother had lived to age 94 and so he figured he had a long number of years left in his retirement to spend with his grandchildren and with his hobbies, which included wood working and stamp collecting for which he had not had time when he was still working. All in all, not a bad outcome!

Recovery from a Heart Attack

It would be hard to say whether the occurrence of a stroke or of a heart attack is scarier: Both have the possibility of sudden death, though most stroke and heart attack victims survive if properly treated.

A heart attack occurs when one of the arteries supplying blood to the heart itself becomes blocked. This leads to sudden chest and arm pain and to heart failure. Again, time is of the essence in bringing the patient to medical attention where he or she can be treated and monitored, and the extent of the cardiac damage can be assessed.

Heart attacks are associated with so-called cardiovascular risk facts: diabetes, high blood pressure, overweight, irregular heart rhythm, among others. The patient may or may not be aware of these risk factors, depending on the kind of medical care he or she has been receiving.

Joseph's Story:

Joseph was a 69 year old insurance salesman who had just retired from his very competitive and stressful job. At 248 pounds he was distinctly overweight, got short of breath when he had to climb a flight of stairs, and avoided taking any long walks. His doctor had told him to "lose weight" a year ago, without any specifics, so it had no effect. As he was cleaning out his file cabinets he developed a sharp chest pain as well as pain in his right arm, and rightly suspected he might be having a heart attack. A colleague drove him to the nearest emergency room where a cardiogram confirmed that he has just had a heart attack. He was admitted to the hospital from the emergency room for bed rest and anti-coagulation.

On further examination he was found to have high blood pressure and occasional skipped heart beats which would require additional attention. He was placed on anti-hypertension medicine. He was again told to lose weight, without further specifics, but this time Joseph took this advice to heart. In fact, he took his heart attack as a wake-up call. He decided to change his life style, for the better. Previously a social drinker, he gave up alcohol. He decided to lose weight, by using a very simple formula: No sugar, no wheat. He began a regular program of exercise.

He began to lose weight, religiously avoiding desserts, breads, cookies, and such, and within six months had come down to a weight of 180 pounds which he had not seen since his college days. He required a new wardrobe, sending his old clothes to the local Good Will store for a tax credit. He felt like a new man!

The Silver Lining in Joseph's Story

The silver lining in this story is pretty easy to find: Joseph became a new man, as a consequence of his heart attack, as a result of his decision to change his life style to a far healthier one. It took active steps and determination to accomplish this, but in this case, he was better off after the heart attack than before.

Recovery from Loss of Hearing

Loss of hearing is most commonly an occurrence in old age, although traumatic loss of hearing can occur at any age. The adjustments needed are similar in either case. We are first going to discuss the impact of loss of hearing on the affected person. Towards the end of this topic we are also going to discuss the impact of loss of hearing on family members and other related persons.

We can deal here only in the broadest terms with all the aspects of hearing loss. This will in addition require consultation with Ear, Nose and Throat specialists, audiologists, and hearing aid experts. However, we wanted to bring this important topic to your attention.

In most people hearing loss comes on gradually and tends to be progressive. Hearing is critically important in relating to and communicating with other people, especially people in one's own household. The goal is to *restore* hearing capability to the maximum degree possible. This can be done through the use of hearing aids of increasing strength and capability. Sometimes there is considerable resistance to acquiring hearing aids. This may lead to arguments with family members about whether hearing aids are needed or not. This, of course, is just a form of denial which many people may use. But hearing aids can definitely improve the quality of communications and the quality of life. When hearing aids no longer work, such drastic measures as cochlear implants need to be considered. A cochlear implant is a surgical procedure to improve hearing. When even these techniques fail, the person with the hearing loss and others in the household may wish to acquire sign language skills.

Which brings us to a discussion of the impact of hearing loss on other members of the person's household. The impact on a spouse or other family member may be as serious as that on the person himself or herself. They may be faced with being asked to repeat almost everything they say to the person which can certainly be annoying; but showing annoyance will only make things worse. A great deal of patience will be required on all sides to cope with progressive hearing loss.

Apart from the impact of hearing loss on the life of the household, the loss will also impact outside communications, social gatherings, musical events, church services, the use of the telephone, watching television and/or movies. Again, hearing restoration through the available means will minimize the damage in these situations as well.

Recovery from Loss of Vision

Loss of vision is also primarily a manifestation of old age, although as with hearing, loss of vision can also occur at younger ages. Accordingly we will again discuss the impact on the older person first, whether it be from old age, a medical illness such as diabetes or hypertension, or an accident or injury.

Again, as with the topic of hearing loss, we can only cover this topic in the broadest terms. Consultations and treatment by ophthalmologists, internists and opticians will also be needed.

The impact of the loss of vision will vary according to the severity of the loss and whether one or both eyes are affected. A first step will be to correct any medical conditions related to the loss of vision. A second step is to determine whether cataracts are responsible. Cataracts can be managed fairly easily these days through cataract extraction.

Corrective lenses or glasses are of course the next thing to consider. These need to be individually fitted, and may be different for each eye.

When no vision can be restored the person is faced with another level of problems. They may no longer be able to navigate even around their own home safely. So here the impact of loss of vision on other members of the family again comes into play. Again, extreme patience is required.

For those completely blind, additional services are available from the state Division of Blind Services, from local Lighthouses for the Blind, and local Lion's Club Sight Programs.

So, in this chapter you have seen recovery from four different physical ailments. All required work, hard work indeed. But reasonably good outcomes resulted. I think you are beginning to see what is involved in recovering from adverse events.

Now on to our next topic: Recovery from mental illness.

CHAPTER 6

RECOVERY FROM MENTAL ILLNESS

The occurrence of mental illness, (depression, anxiety, schizophrenia, alcoholism or other mental disorder), requires treatment and recovery as well. The goal again will be full recovery, if at all possible, or at least substantial recovery to full or near-full functioning. The fortunate part is that most health insurance companies now cover mental illness treatment on a par with physical illness, so lack of coverage for treatment should not be an obstacle to seeking full recovery.

You must start with an accurate diagnosis, for which an evaluation with a psychiatrist is recommended. This will determine what kind of therapies are best applied, including psychotherapy, psychotropic medications, or yet other techniques. Mental illness is equally treatable to physical illness, once the right diagnosis has been established and the right treatment performed.

Depression

Depression is the most common of the mental disorders to occur in adult life. Its symptoms include sadness, tearfulness, and loss of interest, loss of energy, disturbed sleep and broadly-based negativism. Patients may also have suicidal ideas or suicidal plans which need to be carefully evaluated. Depression can be due to any of the adverse events already discussed, or in patients aged 65 and over, it can occur as a biological fact without adverse events. It is also the most treatable of all the mental illnesses. If the depression is caused by an adverse event, psychotherapy and antidepressant medication both are recommended. And sometimes hospitalization is required, especially if suicidal impulses are very strong. The newer anti-depressants are probably more effective than the older ones such as Prozac. Where there is no specific event to trigger depression, but only age, antidepressant medication alone can do the job. However, in some cases, when there is incomplete response to the antidepressant medication, a drug like Abilify, an atypical antipsychotic medication, has been particularly helpful in my practice. Occasionally in severe cases when none of the above approaches work, electroconvulsive therapy may also need to be utilized.

Matt's story

Matt was age 79, a retired married man who went to his primary doctor to complain of depression. He said he was frequently sad, pessimistic, and near tears much of the time. Occasionally he had suicidal ideas but was sure that he would not act on these ideas. The doctor explored what triggering factors (losses, traumas, or disasters) might have befallen Matt, but Matt could not identify any of these. The doctor decided that what Matt suffered from was what he called "biological depression of old age" and that he needed primarily biological treatment rather than a combination of medication and psychotherapy. He decided not to refer him to a psychiatrist but to treat this patient himself, as he was not only an internist but a pharmacologist as well. He prescribed Lexapro, 20 mg per day, and saw him again in a month. Matt was much better but by no means well. His sad mood persisted, becoming particularly pronounced in the late afternoon and evening. He still lacked energy could not interest himself in any activities outside his own home. Accordingly the doctor added Abilify, 5 mg per day for the next two months. This time, when Matt returned he was visibly improved. He smiled a lot and reported that he had begun to volunteer at a clinic for poor people, but suicidal ideas still cropped up from time to time. The doctor increased his dosage of Abilify to 10 mg per day, and with this Matt made a nearly complete recovery from his symptoms. Both Matt and the doctor were satisfied with these results, and the doctor did not try to increase Matt's medication any further for fear of side effects.

Anxiety

Anxiety reactions are also common. The symptoms of anxiety include nervousness, rapid heart rate, fear reactions, and possible gastrointestinal effects. They are most commonly related to adverse events, although they may occur spontaneously as well. A combination of anti-anxiety medication and psychotherapy is the best approach to those situations. It is important to be aware that anti-anxiety medications can be addicting, and long term use of these agents needs to be closely monitored to avoid the complication of addiction.

Alcoholism

Alcoholism is also quite common. It often develops out of social drinking when the individual comes under severe stress or experiences a traumatic event. Alcohol has temporary benefits for both anxiety and depression, but more and more alcohol is needed to allay these symptoms, eventually leading to frank alcoholism. The symptoms of alcoholism include daily drinking to excess or to intoxication or sometimes only binge drinking or weekend drinking. Alcoholics also tend to use devious ways of acquiring alcohol.

To begin treatment the person may first have to undergo supervised withdrawal from alcohol in a mental health setting. Once that has been accomplished participation in Alcoholics Anonymous and psychotherapy and psychoactive medication are recommended. Alcoholics Anonymous acts like a support group and provides a caring and resourceful community to its participants.

Schizophrenia

Schizophrenia tends to be a mental illness with onset earlier in life: the twenties, thirties and forties. If it has been present for a lengthy time, there probably is already a treatment regimen in place. The symptoms of schizophrenia are multiple and well-known. They include so-called positive symptoms, such as delusions and hallucinations. They also include so-called negative symptoms such as social isolation, private meaning in the use of words, and withdrawal from social interaction. A number of newer antipsychotic medications are now available which alleviate both positive and negative symptoms in this disorder. Of particular value in recent years have been long-acting injections of antipsychotic medications that last for up to a month. This approach by-passes the risk of non-compliance with medication-taking.

Post-Traumatic Stress Disorder (PTSD)

PTSD is a mental disorder that some people develop after exposure to a life-threatening even, like combat, or a natural disaster a car accident or rape. Symptoms include anxiety and jitteriness, vivid flashback memories of the traumatic event, disturbed sleep, and inability to concentrate. There may be difficulty in trying to accomplish tasks on the job, or at school, or in social situations. While these symptoms tend to improve somewhat over time, active treatment by psychotherapy and anti-depressant medications is the best approach. Anti-anxiety medications should be avoided since they do not treat the root cause of PTSD and are addicting.

··········

Now you've seen yet another area from which recovery is possible though not automatic. Again, the individual has to seek help in the appropriate places and follow through on advice and directions in order to achieve success. You are beginning to get the idea.

Now we move on to a discussion of recovery from a cancer diagnosis and from cancer treatment.

Chapter 7

RECOVERY FROM A CANCER DIAGNOSIS AND RECOVERY FROM CANCER TREATMENT

My Own Story:

I will now turn autobiographical for this topic. Shortly after my 81st birthday, in October 2016, I discovered a small nodule just below my right jaw. I felt it was a reaction to a local skin irritation I had had. However, over the next three weeks it grew somewhat, became firmer, and became painful when touched. I decided it was time to see my primary care doctor. He examined the area and felt it was "suspicious," referring me to an ear, nose, and throat doctor who saw me the following day. He too felt the nodule was "suspicious" and did a thorough mouth and throat examination. Almost immediately he discovered a lesion on the back of my tongue which he quickly identified as a cancer. WOW! I had not been aware of any abnormality of my tongue up to that point in time. He proposed to do a biopsy of the nodule and did

47

so in the next few minutes, making an appointment for three days hence to come and learn of the results of the biopsy. I came back as scheduled and was told that the lesion was malignant. I HAD CANCER!

Now what? The ENT doctor told me that the site of the cancer way in the back of the throat made the tumor inoperable in view of the many arteries, nerves and other structures in that vicinity. A dual program of radiation therapy and chemotherapy was in order. He had already made an appointment for me with a radiation therapist and an oncologist within the week, and also an appointment for a PET scan to further delineate the site and size of the tumor and any possible metastases to one or more lymph nodes. WOW, again. How is that for life-changing? I know I am not alone in receiving this kind of news. It is repeated daily across the globe.

I first told and discussed this news with my wife. It turned out that through friends of hers who had undergone cancer treatment she was familiar with both the radiation therapist and the oncologist to whom I had been referred, and she had heard nothing but positive things about this treatment team. This was a comfort to both of us. She even knew where their offices were located, fortunately close to home.

Thus began a life-changing period of scheduled treatments, daily (on weekdays) radiation treatments, and weekly chemotherapy treatments. All this was begun after the doctors had made careful calculations as to the amount of radiation and the type of chemotherapy agent to be utilized. All this preparation went smoothly, and treatments were begun in mid-October. A total of forty radiation treatments were ordered and seven weekly chemotherapy treatments. Needless to say, the rest of my usual activities, writing, gardening, and socializing, came to a near halt.

In March of 2017 all active treatments have been completed. Thanksgiving, Christmas, and New Year's all fell within that time period, and no treatments were administered on these holidays. One month from now a repeat pet scan will be performed to see how successful radiation and chemotherapy have been in eradicating the cancer. If any tumor still remains, another form of so-called immunological chemotherapy will be prescribed and administered. Although the specific tumor I had is described by all as "treatable," that is not a guarantee that it cannot recur.

So, on April 14 of 2017 the PET scan of the affected area was completed, and I was given a copy of the disc with the results. My wife emailed the disc to my son who is a radiologist, and by the end of the day he had called me back with the news: "There is no evidence of any remaining cancer!"

A few days later I went back to see the ENT specialist who had first made the diagnosis. He confirmed the findings my son had announced, and also talked with my son by phone right there in the office to make sure they were on the same wavelength. He too seemed very pleased but allowed that while it was good news the possibility of a recurrence was real, and close follow-up, by examination and by imaging studies, would be needed, initially every three months, later every six months. Both my wife and I went home happy.

Now it will be critical not to let fear of a recurrence get the better of me. Nor can I allow myself to become complacent, but must keep everything in perspective. If there is recurrence, additional new forms of chemotherapy are available, based on immunological approaches. But these newer forms of chemotherapy have their own, serious, side effects, altogether different from those of the chemotherapy already administered. So far, so good: I've now had my repeat PET scan of my body and it shows that I am CANCER-FREE. Magic words indeed! A regular series of follow-up visits will now be set up to monitor for any signs of recurrence: failure to thrive, pain, occurrence of a new lump or tumor anywhere inside the body, repeat imaging studies, and blood counts to detect invasion of the tumor to the liver, kidney, bone structure or even the brain. A bit scary, all that, as with all cancers!

At this point in time, nine months after my last treatment (radiation and chemotherapy) I continue to struggle with two problems: The continued loss of taste following treatment; continued weakness and loss of balance, both of which keep me from feeling fully recovered. My wife and I were both reassured and appalled at the same time to hear the ENT doctor describe the treatments I had undergone as "brutal," saying it would take a little more time to regain taste and strength.

I had been told to expect loss of taste as a result of the two treatments, especially as a result of radiation in the neck area. And it did occur so that I could not taste anything, and everything tasted not only bland but awful. I was also told that I could expect gradual recovery from this over the next six months, or over a year's time. That is in fact happening now. I have also regained ten of the twenty pounds of weight I had lost.

In regard to regaining my strength and balance I am now getting physical therapy twice a week, with instructions to work out at home along similar exercises. What has been particularly helpful throughout this experience has been the loving support of my wife and my three sons. Without that I would be having a much harder time dealing with my situation.

I plan to share an addendum, with you the reader, just before this book goes to press, so that you may see how I have coped with my own recovery process.

Some Strategies for Coping with a Cancer Diagnosis

Now I want to discuss some general strategies for dealing with a cancer diagnosis:

Learn as Much as Possible about Your Particular Cancer

Cancers vary widely in their treatability, their aggressiveness, their likelihood for metastases or spreading, their cell type and their location. As always, earliest recognition and early treatment are paramount. You will want to learn signs and symptoms of your particular form of cancer. You will want to learn treatment options, treatment side effects, options for treatment locations, reputation of individual cancer centers and/or practitioners.

The usual methods for treatment are surgery, radiation, and chemotherapy. The type of cancer, its size, location and possible spread, all factor into making a decision. This decision will largely be made by your doctors rather than by you, or in consultation with you, but you should know that each form of treatment has its own side effects, and its own contribution to make concerning the goal of eradicating the cancer. The various side effects of cancer treatment are discussed further in the next section.

Plan to Survive

In the beginning it is best to plan to survive, to "beat cancer." Do not immediately shorten your time horizon, but consider it a warning sign to carefully consider your time horizons in a new light, coming to appreciate all remaining time more than ever before.

Of course there is also the possibility that the cancer may not respond to treatment, or that it will return after treatment. With that it is important to prepare for an earlier departure than you had previously anticipated by "getting your affairs in order." This means reviewing your will and other legal documents, such as power of attorney, and medical surrogate documents. Collect all these in a prominent folder including your computer passwords, bank accounts, investments, and debts, for easy access and review by your survivors and your designated executor.

What is the Silver Lining in this Story?

Early discovery of the tumor is the first of the silver linings in this story. Prompt confirmation of the malignant nature and splendid cooperation between the various doctors involved, and finally, prompt implementation of treatment aimed at eradiating the cancer. Further I had great support from my family and friends, and was able to be pronounced CANCER-FREE at the end of the treatment period. How is that for a silver lining?

Recovery from Cancer Treatment

After coping with the shock of being diagnosed with cancer, and after undergoing whatever treatments are prescribed, the individual now needs to cope with recovering from the treatments for cancer.

All three of the major treatment methods for cancer, surgery, radiation therapy, and chemotherapy, in addition to aiming for the eradication of cancer, have major clusters of serious side effects associated with them. The following are associated with:

Surgery: pain, discomfort, hospitalization, disfigurement, loss of muscle tissue and strength, to name a few.

Radiation: destruction of cells other than cancer cells, such as taste buds, salivary glands, mucosal tissue, gastrointestinal cells and blood–making cells, which could lead to anemia or greater susceptibility to infection.

Chemotherapy: reduction of blood-forming elements including low white cells which increase the risk of infection, low red cell count which produces anemia with consequent weakness, loss of energy, nausea and vomiting, and low exercise tolerance.

All three treatment forms tend to be associated with significant weight loss, but especially radiation therapy to the head and neck region, as it destroys taste buds and makes eating unappetizing. Some of these factors will return to normal functioning, some rapidly, some slowly, some not at all.

Perhaps the most distressing effect of the combination of radiation and chemotherapy is loss of muscle tissue and deconditioning, leading to unsteady gait and generalized weakness. Physical therapy to recover strength in specific muscle groups and to regain balance can be very helpful but must be prescribed by a physician. In addition, a regular routine of walking one to two miles a day is generally recommended. While walking is generally beneficial, it only uses a limited number of muscle groups, and physical therapy needs to be added to retrain all of the muscle groups that have been lying dormant during and after the treatment period.

In addition to regaining energy, strength, and muscle mass, there is the constant concern about the possible return of the tumor. Examining yourself frequently for any new lumps or pains is critical. In addition, the doctor will need to search for any evidence of tumor return, by physical exam and by imaging studies.

A return of the tumor necessitates a whole new strategy to tackle the new cancer growth. In all likelihood, newer anticancer agents using immunologic techniques may be utilized. The longer a patient remains "cancer-free" the better the prognosis. The ideal is to remain cancer-free for the remainder of your life, and eventually die of old age or another illness. Constant vigilance needs to be present, on the part of a patient and on the part of the patient's doctors.

In August 2018 I went to see my oncologist for a follow-up visit. I reported that my energy level had increased somewhat and that I had started physical therapy to regain strength and improve my balance. I also reported that there was further improvement in my taste buds. Laboratory findings showed that there had been no further increase in my hemoglobin level, despite three iron infusions and one injection of Vitamin B12. It was decided to continue one more iron infusion and biweekly B12 injections. The oncologist found me cancer-free!

Can recurrence be prevented?

I had heard and read that there were other forms of chemotherapy available, ones using immune mechanism to treat *recurring tumors. I was curious whether these agents could be used to prevent recurrence. Accordingly I raised the question of possible additional so-called preventive therapy, before there was any sign of cancer recurrence. My doctor expressed a definite opinion that the side effects and risks of such "preventive therapy" were too great, for "someone your age." That put that issue to rest in my mind. If there were recurrence, however, a decision would be made on how to deal with it depending on timing, location, and the issue of spread.*

Another idea I had heard and read about was the use of so-called nutraceuticals – natural agents without serious side effects to try to prevent recurrence. One in particular has been brought to my attention: Curcumin extract, combined with a pepper extract for greater absorption, that has been reputed to prevent recurrence or spread of cancer cells not killed in the first round of treatment. I will bring up this issue with my oncologist the next time I see him, and I plan to follow his advice, for or against. In the meantime I continue with strengthening exercises, balance exercises, Vitamin B 12 injections, regular walking at a brisk pace, and attempting to foster an attitude of alertness but not preoccupation with the issue of recurrence.

It is also important to take a break or a vacation from the recovery process. A week away in a positive setting – the beach, Hawaii, Cape Cod, or the mountains – does wonders for the recovery process, as you will return with renewed energy and zest to your recovery activities. Pleasure produces more pleasure, and pleasurable activities produce more self-confidence and enthusiasm, which is much needed for all the arduous steps of recovery from cancer treatment.

What is the Silver Lining in this Story?

Gradual recovery from all of the side effects of the cancer treatment is taking place. My ability to taste food again is returning. My energy level is increasing. I am regaining most of the weight that I lost during the cancer treatment. So far, all is well.

I have also been able to maintain a positive attitude throughout this ordeal and have come to appreciate the value of my time remaining ever so much.

Now you see that even one of the scariest of illnesses, cancer, can be dealt with, more or less successfully. Again many specific steps need to be taken to accomplish this, plus some of the general supportive steps we have described in Chapter 3.

We next go on to a discussion of one of the other most feared diagnoses: Alzheimer's disease, and its impact on the caregiver.

CHAPTER 8

RECOVERY FROM A LOVED ONE'S ALZHEIMER'S DIAGNOSIS

When a spouse, a parent, or a sibling is diagnosed with Alzheimer's disease, a decision must be made as to who will assume the primary caregiver role. If you are the one taking on the caregiver role, a mountain of responsibilities and demands comes with it. The extent of your commitment and the stress it will produce will only gradually become apparent. If you are not taking on the primary caregiver role, a number of demands and responsibilities will still come your way, but they will only be a mild edition of what the primary caregiver faces. Accordingly our focus here will be the primary caregiver.

First of all, you want to obtain an accurate diagnosis for your loved one with memory problems. Is it Alzheimer's disease or is it another form of dementia? Or is it a reversible dementia, such as from a medication side effect? For this, *get thee to a memory specialist or a memory disorder clinic!* Facilities like these will generally have a whole team of nurses, psychologists, and social workers to assist them in diagnosing and planning for the treatment of an Alzheimer's patient. They will also be best able to serve you, the caregiver.

Early on, try to find out from the memory specialist or memory disorder clinic whether your patient is progressing slowly or rapidly. Alzheimer's can last anywhere from two to twenty years, and you want to have an estimate of how long you may be in the caregiver role.

One additional advantage of working with a memory specialist or memory disorder clinic is that these are the places where clinical trials of new and additional medications are being conducted. The currently available medications – including Aricept and Namenda – are certainly helpful in slowing the progression of the disease, but they are in no way curative. Your loved one may have an opportunity to try newer medications and or procedures.

Barry's Story

I first met Barry in my memory disorder clinic. Barry was a vigorous-looking man with flaming red hair, with a little bit of gray creeping in at the temples. However the most remarkable thing about his appearance was that he carried a very large briefcase in his right hand which weighed his right shoulder down considerably. As he came into my office and sat down, he placed his briefcase prominently between the two of us, emphasizing its importance. I couldn't help but ask him what was in his briefcase. He answered with a single word, "Alzheimer's." He then opened the briefcase and showed me paper after paper on the announced topic, papers from the Journal of the American

Medical Association, Parade Magazine, the AARP Journal, and Xerox copies of articles including Alois Alzheimer's original 1907 article describing the disease for the first time. I was impressed. I looked at him quizzically and he explained. His primary care doctor had made a diagnosis of Alzheimer's on his wife Jeanne and had advised him to become knowledgeable about the disease. He had been told he would be a caregiver for a long time, and needed to be prepared with a full cache of knowledge about the various stages and phases of the disease. I felt my work was half done for me and my team. I couldn't have advised him better myself.

As Jeanne's disease progressed, he had to do more and more things for her: help her get dressed, take her to the bathroom on a regular schedule, prepare simple meals for her and so on. He knew what he was in for from all of his reading. When friends asked him why did not have her admitted to a care facility he replied: "As long as she still knows that she and I belong together, I'll take care of her here."

Eventually the time came when he had to admit her to the memory care unit of the local nursing home. However, he continued to visit her on a daily basis, helping her eat her food, go from her bedroom to the living room and commenting on how pretty she still looked. He saw to it that she had her hair done on a regular basis, and spoke to the nursing staff when there was anything he thought she needed. She no longer recognized him when he came, but he continued to visit regularly as clockwork. He was asked why he still came to see her when she no longer recognized him. He said: "But I still know her." Barry was a model caregiver until the end which came two years after she went to the nursing home.

What is the Silver Lining in this Story?

Actually, there are a number of positive things in Barry's story. First, he made himself thoroughly knowledgeable about Alzheimer's disease. This helped him to be a model caregiver. Second, he provided for his wife the best treatment program available at that time. Third, he was proud of the role he played in supporting his wife in her illness. Fourth, he did not allow himself to be completely consumed by his caregiver duties but maintained social contacts with relatives and friends. Finally, he became involved in supporting research on Alzheimer's disease.

· · · · · · · · · ·

Here you have seen another adverse event, having one's spouse diagnosis with Alzheimer's disease, managed with grace and creativity. You are learning more and more both about a variety of adverse events, as well as about strategies for recovery. Good for you!

In the next Chapter we are going to discuss a very big topic with many variations: Recovery from the death of loved ones.

CHAPTER 9

RECOVERY FROM THE DEATH OF LOVED ONES

A Generalized Approach to Recovery from the Loss of a Loved One

Before going on to discuss the specific adjustments a bereaved person needs to make to the loss of a loved one, let me call your attention to the generalized approach to recovery from any adverse circumstances that we discussed in Chapters 2 and 3. Here is a quick summary of the steps it would be good to take, in addition to the specific steps to be taken to deal with the loss of a loved one. We will review these steps only in this section, but please apply this review of general approaches to all the other losses and life changing events we will discuss.

Begin with an objective assessment of the extent of the loss; commit to a full plan of recovery; maintain good health, good mental health and good social connections. Then follow the advice offered in Chapters 2 and 3.

Specific adjustment to sudden death of a loved one

Loss of a loved one, especially when unexpected, can be one of the most life-changing events. The nature of the loss, and the circumstances surrounding the loss, tend to shape the response of the individual to the event. There are losses for which the individual needs to take no responsibility. They are seen as externally imposed. In some other losses the individual may question his or her own responsibility for the loss. Wasn't there wasn't something more they could have done to prevent the disaster. This may be so whether the loss is from a heart attack, a stroke, an auto accident, or other unpredicted disaster.

Then there are the specific steps which a bereaved person needs to take to recover from the loss of a loved one:

a. Accepting the loss of a loved one as a fact.
b. a certain amount of grieving needs to be allowed and experienced. This is best done with the support of a trusted family member or friend, a confidant, or even a professional counsellor.
c. Finding a way to memorialize the loved one.
d. Looking to see who could now fulfill some of the roles the loved one played in his or her life.

Alexander's Story

The softness of new affection still lingered between Alexander and Jane after all these years. They looked into each other's eyes like love-struck teenagers. They married with the hope of a life together and kept the fire between them burning for 42 years.

They loved to travel. It refreshed his mind to take their vacations together and get away from the legal field where he practiced as an attorney. Jane found the study of human nature to suit her and she became a psychologist. They combined their talents and made a wonderful economic world for themselves which allowed for some extravagant travels. One such adventure took them to South America and the Antarctic. They wanted to see the penguins and experience them up close.

They did in fact find a colony of penguins and they also saw a poignant sight: One lone penguin standing off alone. Wings drooping as if in despair; he had lost his mate. They took a picture of him as it moved them to tears. This lone bird, standing at the seashore, looked out to see a departing ocean liner. They were both impressed with the "humanity" of the bereaved animal and they both treasured the picture.

Back on the ship they were dressing for dinner when Jane fell ill and thought it best to rest. She spiked a fever causing Alexander alarm. He watched over her as she was dripping with sweat and yet shivered with chills. He took her to the infirmary and she was diagnosed with a burst appendix. The infection spread quickly throughout her body and Alexander sat by her bed and talked to her in loving whispers trying to keep her with him. The ship staff tried every antibiotic on board, but what she really needed was to be helicoptered to a mainland hospital. The clock was noted at 11 minutes after ten when she passed.

Alexander was forced to leave the room and waited outside patiently praying with his arms folded like a three-year old boy. He hadn't prayed in years but the occasion called him back to his early childhood when he used to pray, and he found comfort in this action. His life changed in seconds. She was gone. He was numb. That's how it plays out. They tell you something you cannot apprehend and your mind, mercifully, shuts down, and shuts you out of reality for a time. Coming back into reality as the weeks passed he was filled with self-blame and musings about what he could have done differently to avert the tragedy. He stared at the photo of the lone penguin every day, and read the poem he had written for the photo, "Left Behind."

Left Behind
You were
The world to me
Left behind
An ocean of grief

He tried to go back to work. However, he could not concentrate and over a period of several weeks decided to retire from his law practice as he was near retirement age. Thus his grief continued. He experienced sleeplessness, lost interest in food and in other activities, and became a virtual recluse. He did not seek professional help but felt he should be able to cope with his loss. At the same time he felt his wife was totally irreplaceable. Gradually he improved somewhat, began to read classical literature and poetry, and tried his hand at writing poetry himself and found he had a real talent. From time to time he looked at the photograph of the lone penguin and wept.

Clearly, Alexander could have benefitted from a professional mental health counsellor or this book.

Where is the Silver Lining in this Story?

It may be difficult to find a silver lining in this particular story. But it is not impossible to do so. There is the fact that they shared a wonderful life together. Alexander remembered some of their best events together with great pleasure. At the same time, these thoughts kept him from ever considering another liaison later on in life, as he did not think he could find anyone that met the high standards of the relationship he had with his late wife. Although his retiring isolated him somewhat, he did push himself back to activities he had loved before. And he found new skills.

Coping with not One but Two Losses in Succession

While Alexander's story illustrates the difficulty of recovering from the sudden loss of a loved one, our next story shows the impact of more than one loss, under vastly different circumstances.

Melissa's story:

Melissa was married to Ralph, a physician. They lived happily together and had an active social life. They had two children who were becoming independent. Life was sweet. They went on trips. They went on a trip to Mexico City. Ralph developed asthma there and then pneumonitis. They came home but his pulmonary symptoms persisted; in fact, they got worse. He was treated with antibiotics and asthma medications, but he continued to cough frequently and was often short of breath. Within a month Ralph was dead.

Melissa was devastated. She went into social isolation, saw no one; she cried often. Ralph had been a wonderful husband. They had truly loved each other.

But gradually she began to resume social contacts, went to a few parties where she met Jeffrey. At a height of six feet, three inches, a weight of 250 pounds, and with a garrulous personality, Jeffrey was bigger than life. He fell in love and declared his love for Melissa, proposed to her, and she accepted. They lived in a grand house, bordering the golf course. They could play golf anytime right out their back yard. Jeffrey was an investment counselor. He was very successful. He invested money that returned money to the investor at a high rate. He invested money for his friends and Melissa's friends. Only one problem: He was running a Ponzi scheme. When that became known his friends and her friends descended on him with recriminations and accusations, and demands to have their money back. But there was no money to repay the investors. The money had all been paid out to attract new money.

Jeffrey went out on the golf course, just outside the house. He shot himself in the head, as he could not face dealing with the problems he had caused. Thus, Melissa was widowed a second time within a few short years. She moved away from her community, in order not to have to deal with old friends in her bereavement. It took a long time for her to recover, but she was never quite the same. Unfortunately, she did not ask for any professional help but tried to pick herself up from the floor of her despair. Occasionally one of her old friends would go to visit her in her new location. She was friendly, appreciative and kind, but she did not resume an active relationship with anyone.

Another marriage was out of the question for her. She was only sixty years old, still very attractive, but deeply wounded. She did, however, maintain strong relationships with her children and their children. She moved to a beautiful coastal area, interested herself in nature, and involved herself in her new community. Thus she withstood two losses, but with deep scars and some restrictions in her life style.

In this part of this Section we will discuss a number of additional adverse events more briefly. Not that these events are any less important or less impactful. Rather, you can apply some of the lessons learned in the earlier topics to the remaining topics here. So, to begin with do a thorough assessment of what has been lost and what has NOT been lost. Count the blessings that remain and express gratitude for those. Apply the general supportive strategies discussed in Section Two. And as always, look for the silver lining!

Loss of an Adult Son or Daughter

The loss of an adult son or daughter can be particularly hard to bear. This is so for many reasons, a drug overdose, suicide, or automobile accident. Parents often question what they could have done to prevent the tragedy.

Henry's Story

Henry was the middle of three children, having an older and a younger sister. He was a son of a professional couple, he a banker, she a certified public accountant. The children attended private school through high school, and then completed college at a prestigious northeastern college. All three excelled in school and were the pride of their parents. His older sister wanted to become a nurse, and did so. His younger sister was still exploring her options as to a career or motherhood or both. Henry aspired to become a doctor. In fact he had just been admitted to medical school about a month ago, for the next year beginning July 1.

Henry was killed in a head-on collision as he was driving on an interstate near his home town. He was hit by a car headed South in the Northbound lane, and both he and the wrong-way driver were killed instantly. The parents were shocked and devastated. They could not understand why their brilliant son had been taken away from them. They could blame no one else except the wrong-way driver who was also dead. Their grief was indescribable. It was as though their lives had ended. The sisters were equally stunned. They could not attend work or school for the next few days, while funeral preparations were made. There were voluminous expressions of sympathy, both public and private, which did little to console the bereaved.

Is there a silver lining?

It would be difficult to come up with a silver lining in this story. Yes, they still had two healthy children who would probably become even more careful in their driving. Their religious beliefs did not comfort them in this deep injustice. Their well-placed hopes for Henry's and their future together were shattered. There was no possibility of "replacing" Henry, as you might seek to do after some kind of loss. They took comfort in the kind of success that Henry had been until this tragic event. But the wounds ran deep.

Eventually, they would come to accept Henry's death as an unalterable fact. But their lives were never complete again. Loss of an adult child is one of the hardest things for anyone to bear.

Loss of an Unborn Child

The loss of an unborn child is somewhat difficult to imagine. The child has not been born yet, but it clearly has a hold on the prospective parents. It may not have a name yet, and possibly no gender. But expectations run high, and anticipation is great.

In regard to this topic I am going to use two stories to illustrate all that is involved.

Zoe and Johnnie's Story

Zoe and Johnnie were lovers. They were both in their early twenties. He worked for an insurance company; she was a sales clerk at the local dry goods store. They considered becoming engaged but somehow didn't get around to actually make it happen. Then Zoe became pregnant. They were both delighted and it brought them closer together, to the point where they actually became engaged. They each wanted to become the best parents possible to their as yet unborn child. The each beamed when they talked about Zoe's pregnancy.

However it happened that as Zoe was beginning to "show" her growing belly, a large farm dog jumped on her belly and may have caused damage to the pregnancy. In any case, within a week after the incident, Zoe had a miscarriage. Shock and consternation all around! The grief seemed unbearable. Zoe and Johnnie tried to comfort each other, as did the two sets of parents involved. But for the couple this seemed the worst of times they had ever experienced. Their dreams of raising a beautiful child together had been shattered, even before they could begin any parenting.

In the midst of their grief they decided to get married, as soon as possible, but with all pomp and circumstance. They picked a date some three months hence so that all the preparations could be made and all the invitations sent out to family members and friends, far and wide. Amazingly, this seemed to still their grief, or lessened it in any case. They could now think of having future children together once married, and apply the same dreams to those children, as yet nonexistent.

The responses to their wedding invitations came fast and plentiful. Many of the responses included gifts to help them get started in their new life together. The loss of the unborn baby had certainly brought them closer together and closer to their respective families.

The Silver Lining

The silver lining in this story is pretty clear. It brought the couple much closer together. It roused the sympathy of all those around them. Zoe and Johnnie made definite plans to get married, setting a date and sending out invitations. It would be incorrect to say that their grief was resolved, but it was certainly mellowed by the resolute actions they took.

And here is another story of the loss of an unborn child:

Jane and Johnathan's Story:

Jane and Johnathan married relatively late in life. She was in her late thirties, he in his early fifties. Each had devoted their earlier lives to the pursuit of challenging careers, hers as a financial consultant, he as an actor. They were hopeful of having a child or children but for three years there were no results despite on-going attempts. Then Jane missed a period and went to see her doctor. She found out she was indeed pregnant and joy ensued all around, among friends and family. As the pregnancy proceeded Jane had the usual amount of side effects, nausea and fatigue. They were eager to learn the sex of the child and had sonograms done. It was a girl! BUT in addition to learning the sex of the unborn child they also learned that the fetus had multiple congenital abnormalities: two clubbed feet, an atrophied arm, and possible microcephaly or small size of the head. They were stunned. They had known of course that their relatively older age brought with it the possibility of some fetal abnormality, but to have it actually happen! They consulted with numerous doctors, most of whom advised terminating the pregnancy. What a heart-wrenching choice.

Jane and Jonathan took their time making a decision. But after four weeks of painful contemplation, they decided to accept the doctors' recommendation for termination of the pregnancy. That was hard. They grieved, and wondered what else they could do. They finally decided they would adopt an unwanted child, and after qualifying with the adoption agency, they adopted a 5 month old girl. They had already picked out a name for the unborn girl, and they gave that name to the adopted girl. They promised to be the best parents possible to her, and at this time, six years later, both parents and the daughter are doing well by all accounts.

The Silver Lining

Jane and Johnathan practiced many of the generally supportive strategies discussed in Chapters 2 and 3 of this book. They found that their grief over the lost child gradually receded. They became an active part of their community, joined a church and participated in charitable activities. They adopted a little girl and became wonderful parents to her. Well done!

Loss of a Loved One through Murder

Of particular impact can be the loss of a loved when it occurs as a result of murder. This is so regardless of whether the victim was targeted specifically or died as a result of a robbery attempt or of a drug deal gone wrong. Here is one example of such a situation:

Dr. Hanson's Story

James Hanson, a doctor, came home one afternoon only to find his home in disarray and his wife of 22 years murdered. Police were called and an investigation was conducted at the end of which the authorities felt the wife was a casualty coincident to a home break-in, and that his wife had not been targeted by anyone known to the wife or by any known enemy.

Needless to say the impact on Dr. Hanson was devastating. For a while he continued to work on a regular basis, but felt his attention was no longer on his work. He searched his mind as to whether they should have lived in another neighborhood, or another city, where crime was less likely, or whether he had failed his wife by not providing a home security system. At times he even felt that other people considered him a suspect in arranging the murder, although they had been happily married. He decided to give up his medical practice and half-heartedly offered consultant services to other physicians, but without much success. He realized he was depressed and consulted a trusted psychiatrist, who discussed his situation with him and prescribed antidepressant drugs. These were of some help, but Dr. Hanson was still a broken man.

Dr. Hanson had been quite a connoisseur of fine cuisine and in fact was co-owner of one of the city's well-known eating establishments. He gave up his interest in fine dining and disposed of his part-ownership of the restaurant. Years later he was still leading a marginal life. His psychiatrist never mentioned the need for a recovery program. He finally heard of a national support program for people who had had similar experiences, and he joined that group and gradually dug himself out of his miserable existence. He took up writing about medical conditions on which he was an expert, and gave lectures to medical and lay organizations. He also moved away from the site of his wife's death, taking up residence in California. Gradually he resumed a full and happy but redesigned life.

Recovery from Loss of a Spouse by Divorce

Since nearly one out of two marriages ends in divorce in the United States it is important to discuss this topic here. Divorces can and do happen, with a variety of impacts on the couple involved. Even a so-called "friendly" divorce can leave in its wake a sea of consequences to which the divorced individual needs to adjust: a loss of companionship; a loss of intimacy; a loss of part of one's social network need not occur if the terms of the divorce are in fact mutually agreeable. Nevertheless, adaptations need to be made to replace the losses that do occur. These will include choices about where to continue to live, whether or what kind of a job to hold, whether or not to try to pursue a new intimate relationship by resuming "dating." Dating is put into quotes because dating after a divorce does not closely resemble dating in one's youth. If the choice is not to seek a new intimate relationship, other adjustments need to be made to meet some of the basic human needs for companionship: finding new friends or strengthening the relationships with family members.

Angela's and Rick's Story:

This is an example of a relatively friendly divorce. Yet major personal pain, financial stress, relocation of housing, and other stresses still occurred:

Angela and Rick were seemingly happily married. They had two children, three years apart, who were intelligent, easy to manage and full of a variety of interests. Then Rick became interested in politics, first at the local level, then at the state level.

Politics took over his life. Angela had no interest in politics and refused to be drawn into his new activities. He, for his part, neglected his wife and children, and soon he was beginning to see other women. Divorce was clearly the next step. This was painful to Angela as Rick had simply "lost interest in her," in favor of politics at which he was quite successful, first as a state representative and later as a state senator. They were divorced, reasonably amicably as far as legal issues, property division and care of their two children was concerned. But the wounds of being rejected were deep for Angela. She had to hold two jobs in order to support herself and help with the children's education, but she managed. She attempted a relationship with another man who was still married but separated from his wife. He was always broke as he had to pay bills and child support for two children, even though he had a professional career as an accountant. Eventually the strain of this relationship was too great, and she decided to "go it alone." In this she was much happier. She took over the running of her family business, a travel agency which was largely run by a very efficient manager, so that she had relatively few responsibilities. Her ex-husband remarried; however, he would visit occasionally, and they agreed on the summer-camps, and after-school programs for their children. So the divorce eventually became just a fact of life for Angela, and she could develop her other interests: teaching and planning child care.

Recovery from an Unwanted Divorce

Most divorces are to some degree unwanted. However, truly unwanted and contested divorces can be real horror stories, involving endless fights between opposing lawyers, fights over child custody, battles over money, over the primary residence, the disposition of household pets, payment of alimony and so on.

Recovery from an unwanted or contested divorce is thus a whole other story. The amount of variability from one case to the next is endless. First there is the rancorous time leading up to the divorce. Then there are the painful after-effects of a divorce: continued recriminations, loss of income, loss of self-esteem, among others.

Need for a confidant

In a contested divorce, both before and after the actual divorce, a confidant is needed by each partner. This could be a family member, a close friend or a professional counselor.

Alternatively, or additionally, participation in a divorce-focused support group may be very helpful for each ex-partner.

Chronicling Your Story

One other technique which has often been helpful in this situation is to chronicle one's own emotional experience, through a diary, or a memoir. At best this might even led to marketing a best seller about one's experience recovering from a divorce, but don't count on it. Short of that, it will give you a better picture of what you are going through.

As I have said, divorce can be hell, as seen in this story:

Janet and Jack's Story:

Janet and Jack were married for twenty years, he an attorney, she an accountant. They had two children, both teenagers. The children, like the parents, were bright intellectually. They were very sociable, with a large social network. Janet and Jack decided to get a divorce, but the reason for their divorce was not entirely clear. It may have involved infidelity on Jack's part, but that was not the public reason for their divorce. They became very angry with each other. Each hired prominent and aggressive divorce attorneys who incidentally hated each other, making negotiations all the more difficult and prolonged. The divorce wreaked havoc on their social lives, as each wished to claim previous associates as their friends, forcing many of their formerly joint friends to take sides. Thus while each clung to their former connections, the two could never be invited anywhere together. Eventually Jack moved away, and married the woman with whom he may or may not had an affair while still married to Janet. The divorce was rough for both Janet and Jack. But their children really suffered the most from the divorce process. Their foundation was shaken by the events and they became unsure of themselves and lost self-esteem. Both of the children required psychiatric treatment.

As to Jack and Janet, they never fully recovered. Jack's new marriage seemed stable on the surface, but there were suspicions that all was not well. Janet never remarried but moved to another city to start a new life. Their wounds ran deep, and both remained bitter when asked about the other person.

Loss of a Beloved Pet

While loss of a beloved pet is not necessarily life-changing, it can have a significant impact of the emotional life of individuals or of a whole family. To start with, they will feel empty or incomplete and feel that their pet cannot possibly be replaced. After a while, however, they may consider adopting a new pet, one similar to the lost animal, or even quite a different type of animal to make them feel whole again.

Cats and dogs, the most common pets in our culture, have a limited life span ranging from perhaps ten to as long as 17 years. Whether the loss occurs through old age, or through an accident or illness, the idea of replacement should never be far from one's mind. It can be very satisfying. Not only can one acquire a new pet as a kitten or a puppy, or one can acquire a grown animal from a pet store, breeder, or from an animal shelter. Most people will want to acquire a pet that has strong similarities to the lost animal, but exploring other possibilities is one of the silver linings of such a loss. Some people explore the use of a similar name. Thus if the lost cat's name was "Boots" the new cat might be named "Boots II."

Again, taking action is critical to coping with this loss as well as with others. Replacement is not always possible, but is more readily so in the case of a loss of beloved animal.

In trying to replace a lost pet, you should think of the various animal shelters that hold rescued animals. Being able to provide a "forever" home can be very satisfying. Other places to consider contacting are "rescue groups" for a specific breed that you are looking for. Thus there are poodle rescue centers, Labrador rescue centers, Siamese cat rescue centers, and so on. Sometimes acquiring a grown pet that needs love and a new home is more satisfying than going through the trials of puppyhood with a new animal. We have several times in our lives acquired adult animals from rescue shelters, and have been very happy with the new family member.

Mimi and Mathew's Story

Mimi and Matthew had a favorite cat, named Molly who was their dear companion for many years. Unfortunately when Molly was 13 she died after a brief illness. Mimi and Mathew were heart-broken. Their friends advised them adopt another cat, but they couldn't envision one who could replace Molly. For a long time they went without a cat. However when they were at someone else's house that had a cat they always took time to find and pat their cat with pleasure. Still, they resisted, weighing up the options of being less tied down.

It then happened that a friend of theirs was given an abandoned cat to take care of. Mimi and Mathew visited the friend and found the cat, Toby, very likeable. They decided they would be willing to take care of it. The cat was used to being an outside cat, and at first did not take well to being cuddled or to lap-sitting. But over a period of several months the new cat became the friendliest of indoor cats, purring when petted, seeking out contact and begging for food. Needless to say that Mimi and Mathew were very glad that they made the move to adopt a new cat.

· · · · · · · · ·

Wow! That was a lot of information to absorb, and a lot of suffering to relate to. But again, the simple message shines through: "You can get over this."

CHAPTER 10

RECOVERY FROM CAREGIVING

As I mentioned earlier, my starting point for this book was my observations of the need for recovery from caregiving, especially from caregiving of an extensive chronic illness or disability. Accordingly I also want to focus on this topic in considerable detail, and then draw parallels to all the other mishaps that can derail one's life.

If you have been a caregiver for someone with Alzheimer's disease or another chronic disabling condition, or if you are nearing the end of your caregiving experience, this is written for you. Until now only scant attention has been paid to that period of life of caregivers when the patient for whom they were caring has died. Yet I think this one of the most important chapters in the complete story of caregiving. In fact, many caregivers cannot imagine a life after their caregiving is finished. However, as one caregiver recently told me unequivocally: "There IS LIFE after Caregiving." I can only agree wholeheartedly.

Accordingly, I want to share with you what I have learned from former caregivers as to what is involved in recovering from caregiving. To be sure, time is a great healer, but please be advised that time alone is not enough. Recovering from caregiving requires a constellation of deliberate and coordinated activities that will pay off handsomely when diligently and thoughtfully pursued.

Your Caregiving Days are Now Over

In this chapter I want to take you by the hand and walk you through what lies ahead. You have completed your caregiving experience and it is now time to resume your own life to the fullest. So what can you expect? And what do you need to do? I think you are going to be amazed.

What is the Silver Lining in your Caregiving Experience?

When you really "wake up" from caregiving you will find that you are now a changed person in a number of ways. These represent the silver linings that have been part of your caregiving experience. Gradually you will realize that:

- You have learned that you can adapt to ever-changing circumstances.
- You have learned that you can be far more creative than you had ever imagined.
- You have learned just how strong and resourceful you are.
- You have learned how to give unconditional love over an extended period of time.

Of course, the exact nature of these changes will vary widely from person to person. You will also discover that you have lived through a lengthy period of severe stress, and that too has left its mark on you. You will discover left-over scars and wounds which need healing. Again, the exact nature of these will vary from person to person. Thus you may from time to time be overcome by strong emotions such as severe sadness, feelings of guilt, anger, or other unwelcome emotions. In some ways these experiences resemble flashbacks such as those experienced in post-traumatic stress disorders. If this happens to you, be assured that you are not alone; many caregivers have told me that they were very surprised when they first experienced these feelings, and they didn't quite know what to make of them. What it means is the long period of stress, isolation, or limiting your personal life to caregiving, has taken its toll. You will now need to drive towards a full recovery from caregiving.

Continue to Participate in Your Caregiver Support Group or Find or Start a Support Group for Recovering Caregivers

In my book "Caregiving in Alzheimer's and Other Dementias (Yale University Press, 2015) I've made the case for belonging to an Alzheimer's caregiver support group. Well, either continuing with your caregiver group or starting a new group for recovering caregivers is a great idea. You may be able to pioneer one such in your community, if none exist, or you may be able to find one though the Area Agency on Aging or through your social network, on Facebook, or on Linked-In. Be bold. You will be thoroughly rewarded for doing so.

What does it take to recover from caregiving?

It actually takes a lot. You will want to undertake a whole set of coordinated activities in order to become "whole" again.

You will want to rebuild your social network. This will involve letting friends and acquaintances know that you are "back"; you will want to become socially more active, attend parties, or perhaps give a party to demonstrate that you are back. And you will start to accept invitations to parties again.

You will want to assure optimal nutrition to support your recovery. This will mean inclusion of lots of fruits and vegetables in your diet, and minimizing anything containing refined sugar or refined flour. You will also need to assure that you have an adequate intake of healthy fats, ample vitamins, and an array of supplements.

You will be able to resume regular sleep patterns, aiming for 7 to 8 hours of sleep, going to bed and arising at the same time each day.

You will want to resume regular exercise activities, preferably with other people rather than alone.

You can practice the stress reductions that work for you, whether these include meditation, yoga or tai chi, or just regular times for deep breathing exercises. Of course spending time with trusted friends whenever new stress occurs will also help. And be assured that new stress will still crop up in your life.

You now have the freedom to seek out pleasurable activities on a regular basis and even indulgences of which you have probably long been deprived.

This is a good time to offer and receive love from friends and relatives. Household pets can also provide and accept unconditional love. Just being next to and petting an animal we love is a great stress reducer and a way to feel good about ourselves.

You can also reconnect with your spiritual life, which, too, may have lapsed during your long period of caregiving. This may include religious or non-religious forms of spirituality, as well as regular experiences in nature. I have long been a believer in the creative and curative benefits of communing with nature.

For some individuals supportive counseling with a mental health professional may be needed. You should not hesitate to access such help if you continue to experience depression or frequent attacks of anxiety.

You Could Apply Your Knowledge of Caregiving to Help Other Caregivers

You might apply the knowledge you have gained to help other people struggling with caregiving tasks. Certainly there is a great need for this; and you would be highly rewarded for teaching others what you have learned during your long career as a caregiver. Or you might become a fund-raiser for Alzheimer's disease research, since you know so well that further progress in this area is desperately needed.

You Could Write a Book about your Caregiving Experience

You could even write a book about your caregiver experience. You would have much to share, and many would be grateful for what they could learn from your journey. An even more interesting variation on this theme might be for you to *write a book about the person for whom you provided care*. Now there is an idea!

You May Wish to Turn in an Entirely New Direction

On the other hand, you may wish to turn completely away from having any further dealings with this disease, and pursue all those activities that had to be back-burnered during your caregiving career. This might include reconnecting with other family members, friends whom you may have had to neglect while caregiving, or to pursuing creative or spiritual activities. A long and a long-delayed vacation would certainly be something you deserve, and which you can now enjoy.

Write Your Future

And I literally mean for you to write your future. It has been repeatedly demonstrated that a written plan is far more likely to be accomplished than is a general idea. Make it as detailed as you can envision it. Then picture it in your mind, not only seeing what you are planning to achieve, but also visualizing how it would feel to execute what you have sketched out. Then start to implement it, one step at a time. Make adjustments in your plans as needed, and overcome obstacles to your plan through persistence and endurance.

As part of this healing process, you may want to establish a whole new set of goals for the remaining part of your life.

What this may include will depend at what stage in life you are when your caregiving is over. If you have been a caregiver for a spouse of a similar age to yours, the time remaining might only be somewhere between five and fifteen years. If you have been caring for a parent, you may only be in your fifties or sixties, and you will have a whole generation of life left to live, anywhere from ten to thirty-five years. So what I recommend is that you first start by making notes of things that occur to you that you might still wish to accomplish or to experience; then begin to prioritize them; then begin to discuss them with family, friends, confidants or counselors, or with individual members of your caregiver group. This will be a most important undertaking for you. What I recommend is that you do in fact sit down and literally write your future.

You are a Modern Day Hero

Whatever activities you may wish to undertake, you will be able to do so with greater skills and confidence than ever before. Nothing could be more difficult than what you have been through. I personally believe that you as a caregiver of someone with Alzheimer's disease have truly been a modern hero or heroine. Congratulations! Well done! You have every reason to be truly proud of yourself. The power of your shining example will be there for others to follow. Thank you. Thank you. I say this on behalf of all the patients who can no longer say it themselves. You can be assured that you can handle anything that happens in the rest of your life.

Alice's story

Alice, age 77, had been a caregiver for over seven years when her husband Bill died of Alzheimer's disease in a nursing home. He had been a brilliant physician who had invented several surgical procedures that were named after him. And it had been painful for Alice to see his amazing mind gradually fade and fade away, to the point where in the last 12 months he could not communicate at all and barely acknowledged Alice when she came to visit. It had been an exhausting time for Alice. She lost weight. She was cut off from her previously active social life. She no longer attended church, did not go out to eat, and led a generally restricted life. Her beautiful shepherd dog Billie went with her everywhere, however, and was her only reliable source of joy and companionship.

Amidst her grief of finally losing Bill, she felt guilty that she also felt some relief that this phase of her life had come to an end. She didn't need to go to the nursing home anymore as she had done on a daily basis. She was free to schedule her time in any way she pleased. However she really did not know what to do with that time after several weeks of taking care of funeral arrangements, death certificate copies, life insurance notification, notification of various family and friends of his death, and responding to expressions of sympathy. She didn't know what to do with the rest of her life.

Gradually, she pushed herself to resume her previous social contacts: long-term friends, a few members of her church, and more outreach to her children. She also returned to writing poetry and joined a local poetry society. At about this time her beloved dog Billie died, primarily of old age. She quickly went *to the local Humane Society and adopted another dog, another but much younger shepherd whom she also called Billie.*

She had kept a diary during her caregiving days. So she tried to make her notes into a full-scale memoir of her time as caregiver and beyond. She was actually able to get the memoir published under the title "My life: An explanation" which sold a few thousand copies and got some very positive reviews.

She was again seen smiling when she walked her dog, stopping to chat with neighbors and friends, and even reaching out to have a party for people she had not seen in a long time. Most important to her, she raised funds for a memorial to her late husband. Thus Alice returned herself to a full life, older but wiser from her caregiving experience.

What else is the silver lining in this story?

Apart from the several positive outcomes already previously mentioned in this chapter, this story reveals a number of additional beneficial outcomes. Alice discovered a whole new talent she did not know she had: writing poetry. After publishing two books of poems she also began to promote poetry in general in her community. She also became an avid advocate for Alzheimer's care and research. Her family rallied around her in recognition of the remarkable caregiver services she had provided. And when her beloved shepherd dog died of old age she dared to reinvest her love by adopting a younger shepherd dog from the animal rescue shelter. Well done, Alice!

. . . .

This brings us to the end of our discussion of major adverse events. Of course we have not covered all that can go wrong in a life time: There is the possibility of war. There is the possibility of losing one's home through a house fire; the possibility of a major automobile accident, with total loss and possible death or injury to one or more of the victims. The list goes on and on.

CHAPTER 11

THE NEXT HORIZON

Dear Reader: We have now come to the end of *Up from Down: How to Recover from Life-Changing Adverse Events.* You are now equipped to handle anything that comes your way. With this book in hand, or rather in your mind, you should be prepared to handle any disastrous event, to bounce back from it, and perhaps go on to a higher level of functioning than ever before.

Up from Down is intended to have an impact on you. It doesn't merely want to be interesting or entertaining but it wants to bring about changes in you, and perhaps through you, in other people. It wants to bring about changes that matter both in the short run and in the long run. It wants to be relevant to your life, now and in the future. It also wants to remind you to continue to look for the silver lining in any loss or trauma, both for yourself and for others in your life.

My wish for you

I wish that from this day forward you will walk without fear into each day, wherever your journey takes you. I wish that you will learn from any failure, large or small. I wish you happiness and gratitude for whatever comes your way. I wish you joy, love, and peace for ever and ever.

My invitation to you

Finally, if and when you run into difficulty and don't know the way out, I want to invite you to write me about it and ask if I can be of help. I do not know how many requests I can respond to, but I will do my best. I have a great deal of interest in your personal experience with adverse events, and would like to learn from them. You can e-mail me with your thoughts and questions at http://epfeiffe@health.usf.edu. I thank you in advance for your faith in me and I thank you for reading *Up from Down*.

AFTERWORD

Now that the book is finished, let me comment on the relationship between my cancer and the creation of this book. While the effects of treatment made it more difficult to write, it also instilled inspiration to absolutely finish this book before all time expired for me. At this point I am cancer-free, and the book is finished.

ACKNOWLEDGEMENTS

I owe an enormous debt of gratitude to the people about whom I have written in this book. Their joys and sufferings were the inspiration for this work.

Then there were other people who helped. Above all my wife Natasha who read every page of this manuscript over and over again, who gave me feedback about what worked and what didn't work; what was clear and what was not clear; what was awkward and what was elegant; what was understandable and what was obscure. She helped make this book accessible to the reader, not a scholarly book for fellow scholars, but for real people going through life-changing events with a guide by their side that had not been available before. I am enormously beholden to her. And she did so with grace and without giving offense so that I could respond positively to her suggestions, rather than be offended or become defensive.

Second, there was my writing coach, Lisa Tener who helped me make the writing flow smoothly, who helped me with organizational issues, so that there was a logical progression to the work. And she helped me to write in shorter sentences which I am sure every reader appreciates.

I also want to thank Dr. Anthony Shaw for allowing me to use his wonderful photograph of the bereaved penguin in the chapter on the loss of a loved one.

I want to thank Rainbow Abegg, Life Coach at Achieve Today, for writing a heartfelt Foreword.

I want to thank Jenny Shepley and Ivy Stirling of Author Bridge Media for outstanding editorial assistance. They helped to sharpen the focus of the book and helped me to make the book more interesting.

Finally, I want to thank all the staff at Balboa Press, from copy editor to designer to publicity which made this all come together into a handsome worthwhile book.

SUGGESTED READING

Adamson, Ted,: *Up from Down: The True Story of Recovery from Addiction, Amazon Books,* 2011.

Kushner, Harold S., *When Bad Things Happen to Good People.,* Schocken Books, 1983.

Kater, Donna H., *I'm Still Alive, Now What?,* Amazon Books, 2016

Loos, Dickson., *Life Changing Event,* Createspace, 2013.

Mongelluso, N.B., *Understanding Loss and Grief, 2013.*

Pfeiffer, Eric: *Winning Strategies for Successful Aging.* Yale University Press, 2013.

Pfeiffer, Eric: *Caregiving in Alzheimer's and Other Dementias.* Yale University Press, 2015.

Sanberg, Sheryl and Grant, Adam: *Option B: Facing Adversity, Building Resilience, and Finding Joy.* Alfred A. Knopf, New York, 2017.

Schiraldi, Glenn R., *The Post-Traumatic Stress Disorder Sourcebook,* 2016.

Stanley, Charles: *How to Handle Adversity.* Grason, Minneapolis, MN, 1987.

Vaillant, George E. *Adaptation to Life,* Little, Brown and Co. 1977.

Van Der Kolk, Bessel, *The Body Keeps the Score: Brain, Mind and Body in the Healing of Trauma,* Penguin Publishers, 2014.

INDEX

N

nature iv, 2, 6, 15, 16, 52, 62, 63, 67,
   83, 85

P

positive attitude 12, 16, 56
PTSD 3, 45

R

radiation therapy 4, 48, 53
recovery xi, xii, xiv, 1, 2, 3, 4, 5, 6, 9,
   10, 11, 12, 13, 16, 18, 19, 27, 29,
   31, 32, 33, 35, 37, 39, 40, 41, 43,
   46, 47, 50, 51, 52, 55, 56, 57, 60,
   61, 73, 74, 76, 81, 83, 84, 97

recurrence 35, 49, 50, 54, 55
retirement 34, 35, 65, 101

S

schizophrenia 3, 41, 44, 45
sex 71
silver lining 6, 8, 21, 35, 37, 52, 56, 60,
   65, 68, 69, 71, 72, 82, 89, 91
social connections 61
spirituality 85
stories xiv, 2, 4, 5, 14, 69, 76
stroke 3, 10, 12, 32, 33, 34, 35, 62
support groups 10

About the Author

Dr. Eric Pfeiffer is a nationally and internationally recognized authority on health and aging. He has written a number of medical textbooks on aging, and since his retirement in 2008 he has been writing a series of books for a lay audience. The most important of these are *Winning Strategies for Successful Aging,* Yale University Press, 2013, and *Caregiving in Alzheimer's and Other Dementias,* Yale University Press, 2015. He has also written a book of poems entitled *Under One Roof,* published by Amazon.com.

He is currently Emeritus Professor of Psychiatry and the Behavioral Sciences at the University of South Florida, College of Medicine. He has an endowed chair named after him for research on Alzheimer's disease at USF, and an imaging center named after him for PET scans in memory disorders and other conditions. He lives in Tampa, Florida. At the time of this writing he is 83 years old.

NOTES

NOTES

NOTES

Printed in the United States
By Bookmasters